KATZ KREATIONS I

A MANDALA COLORING BOOK

Color your way to relaxation
Vol 1

KATHLEEN PRINCE

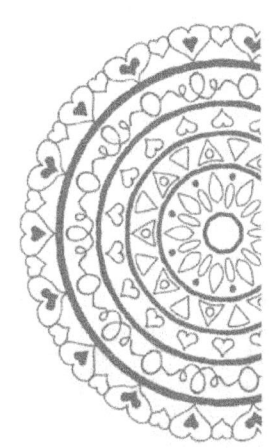

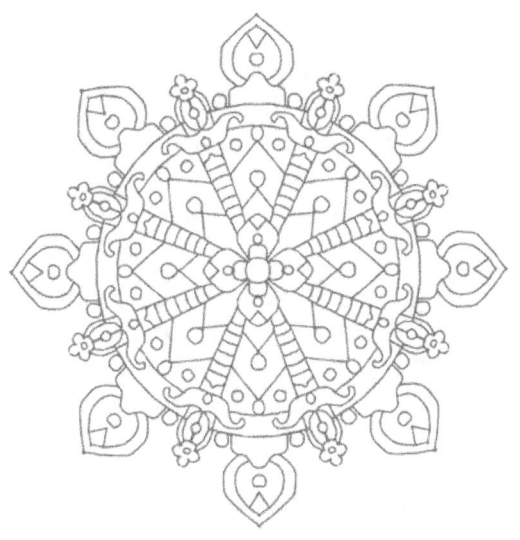

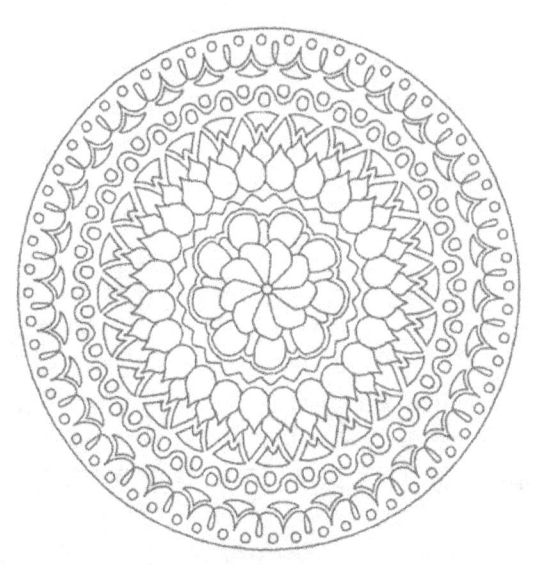

INTRODUCTION

Mandala means "circle", a geometric way to represent the universe and the circle of life.

Although Mandalas have spiritual undertones, the mandalas in this book were created in the hopes that they would bring peace and relaxation to those who might choose to spend some time coloring them in. Whether one uses crayons, colored pencils, pens, markers or paints, the end result will be wonderful. There is no wrong choice of medium to use.

When coloring, don't hold back. If you feel like using bright blue, do it! Feeling quiet? Color with soft muted colors. Don't worry about using the wrong color – just use what feels right to you. Enjoy the journey of completing your colored mandala.

I started out coloring mandalas myself, and found it to be a very relaxing activity. Coloring then led to doodling, which lead, ultimately, to creating new mandalas. All the mandalas in this book are hand-drawn – thus you will notice the irregularities in the circles, lines, etc. To me, that is part of what makes these mandalas unique.

I hope you enjoy the designs in this book, and find yourself relaxing as you put colored pencil to paper and personalize your own mandala.

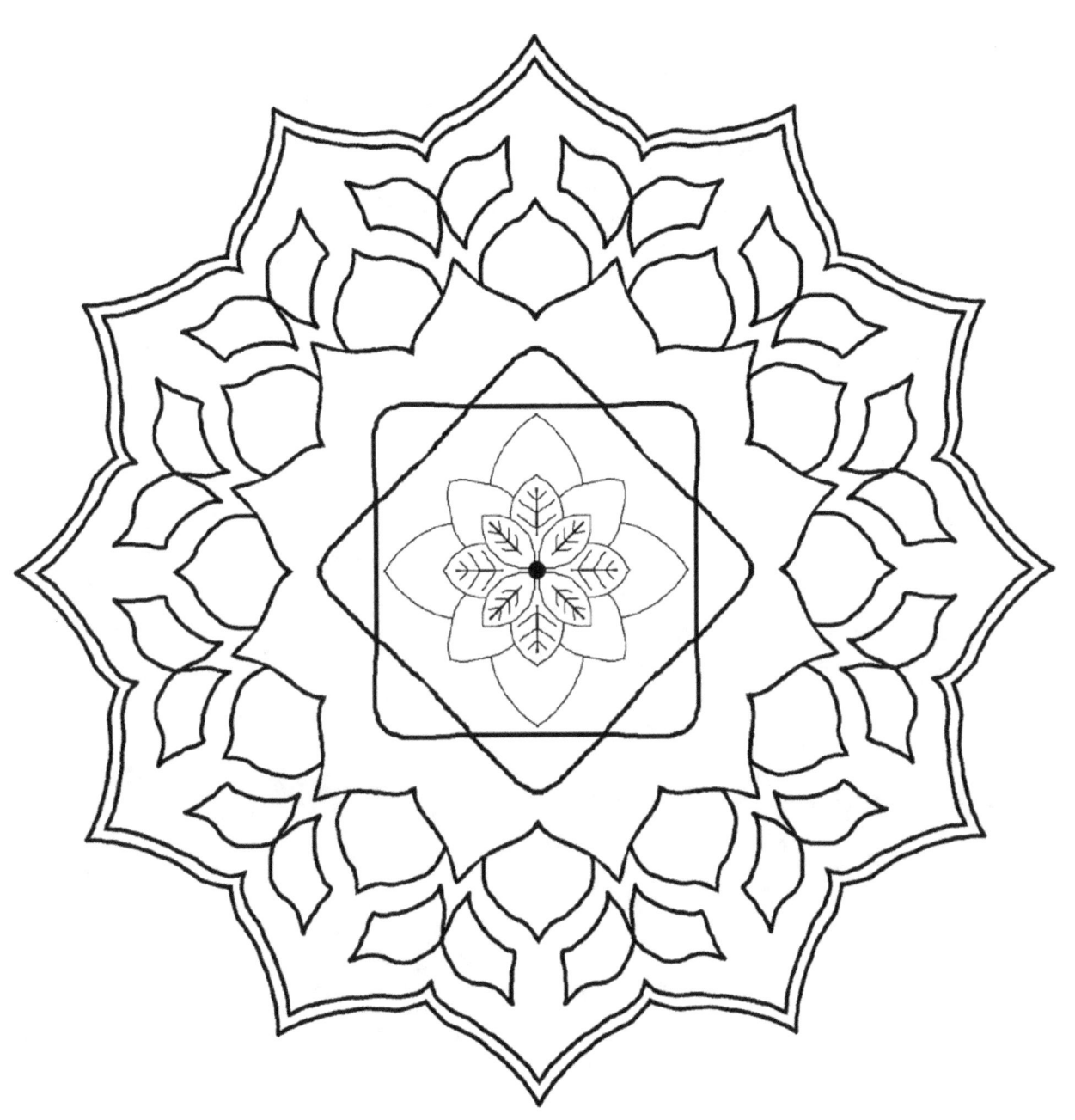

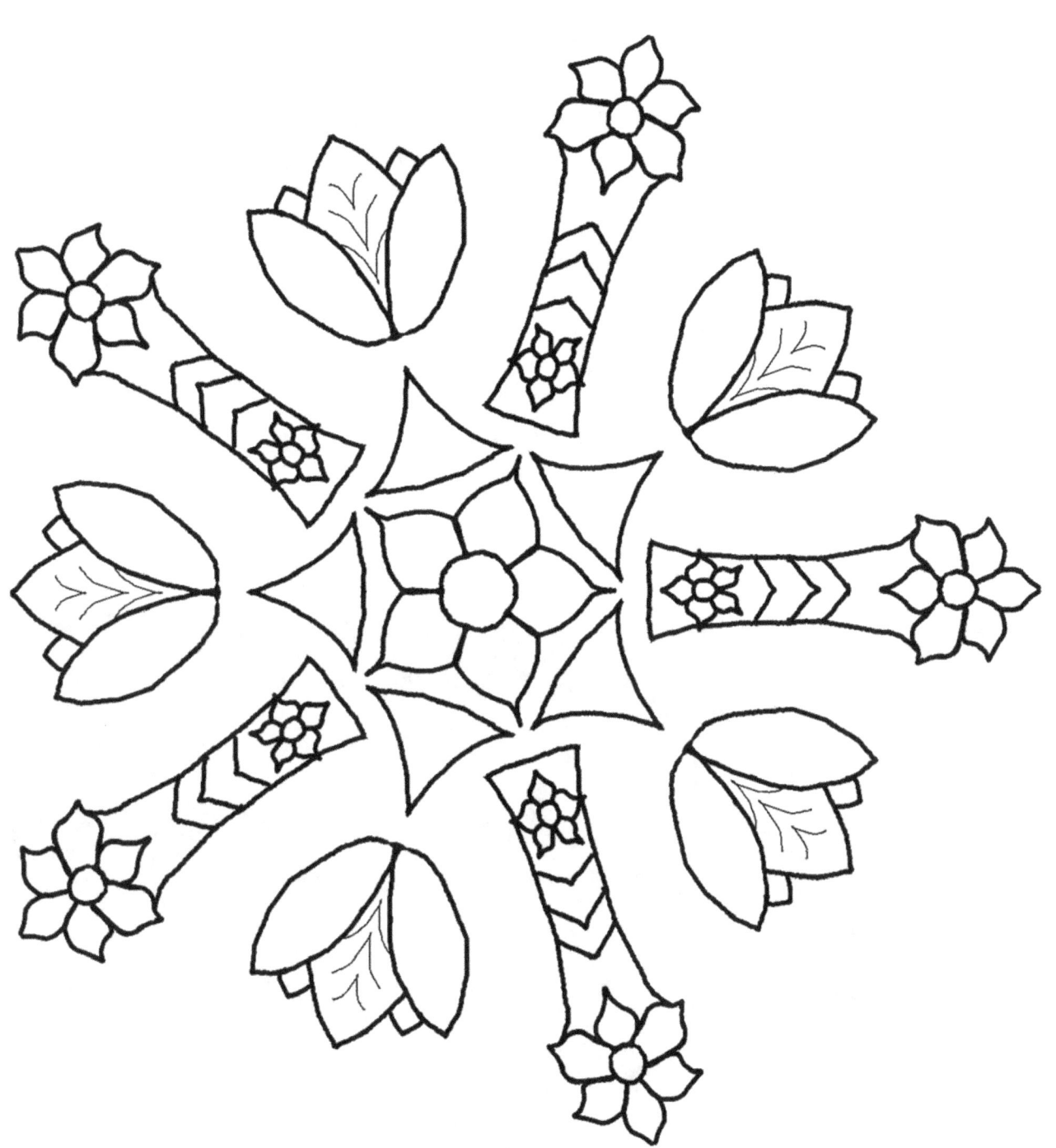

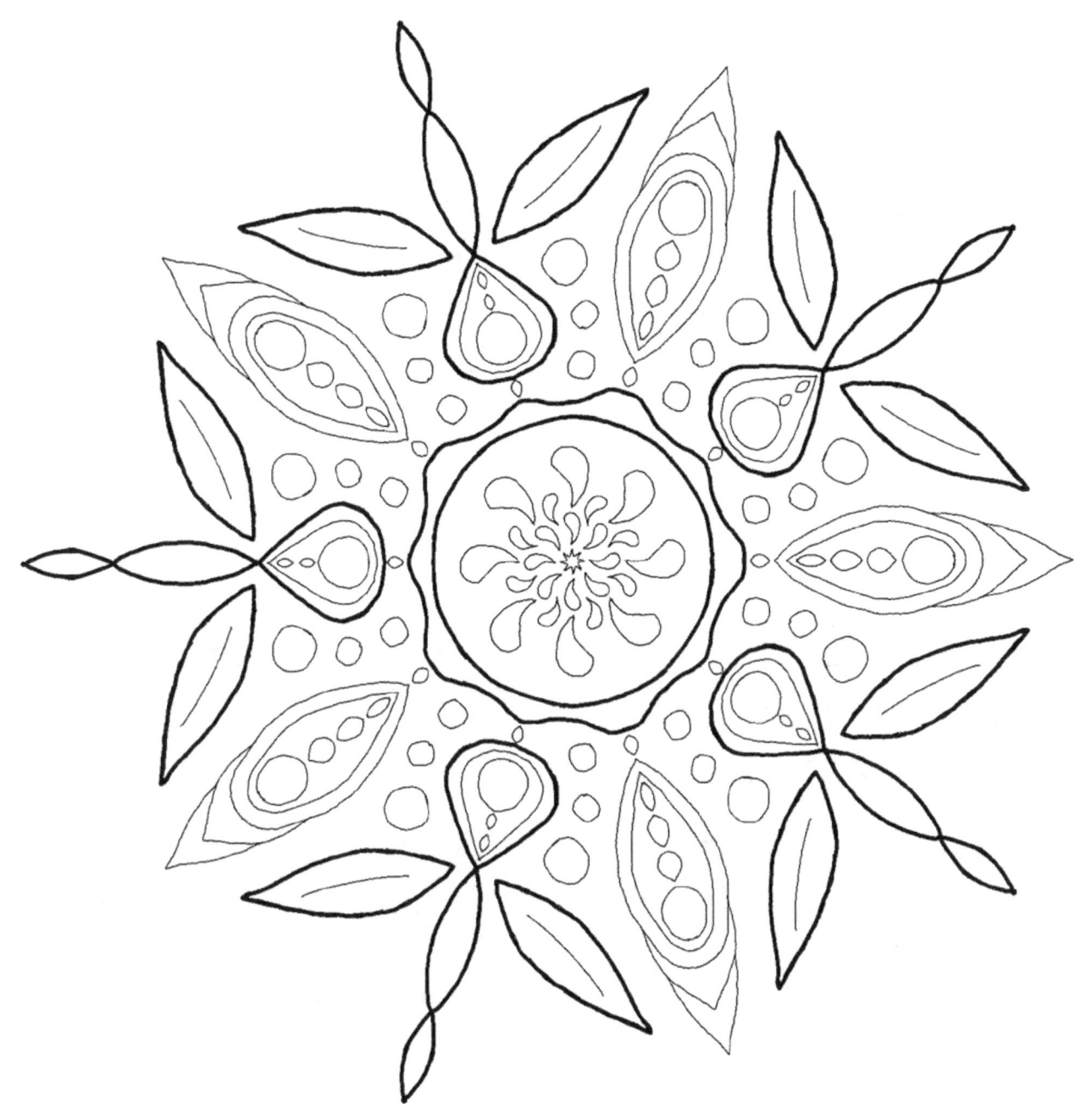

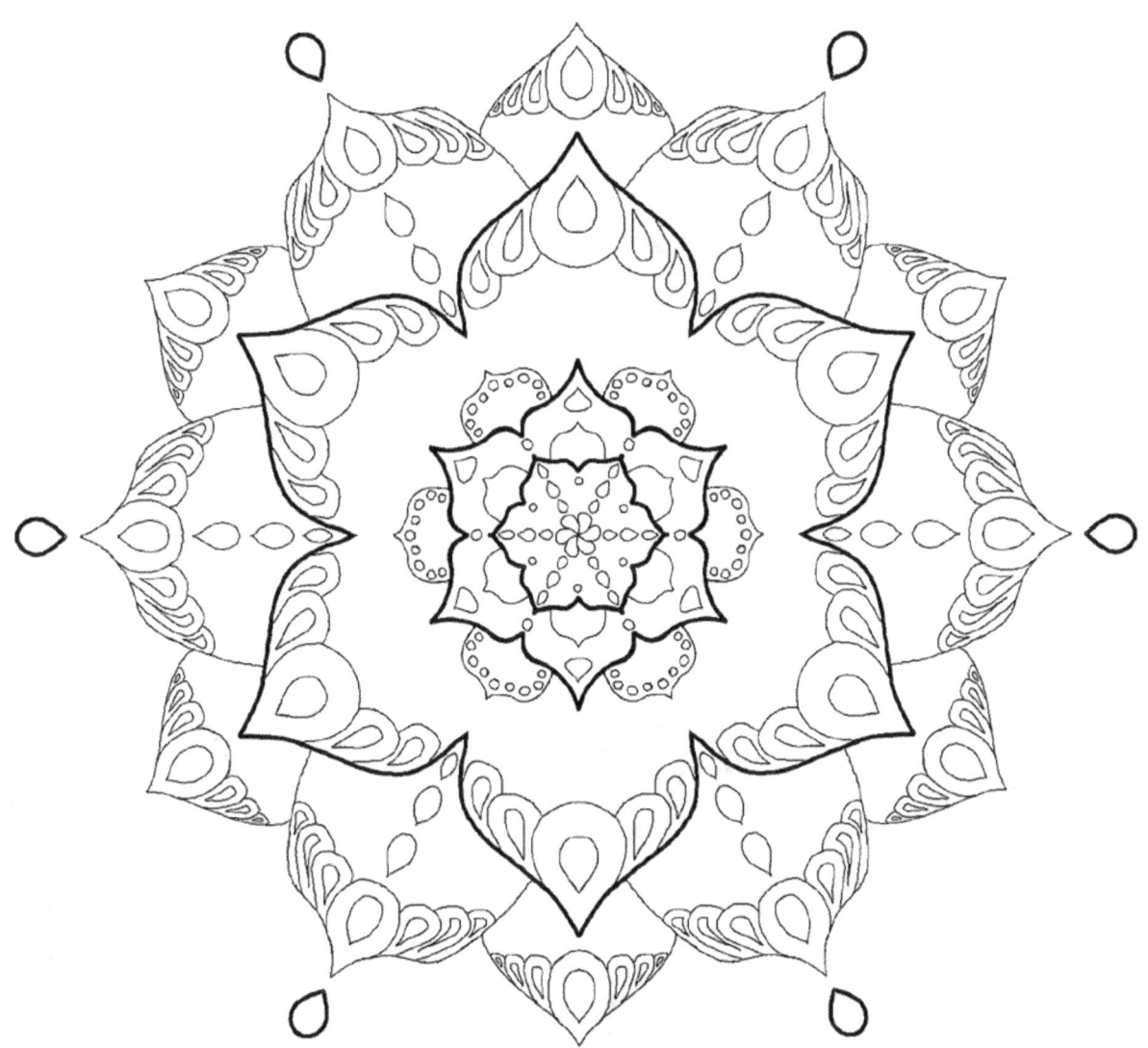

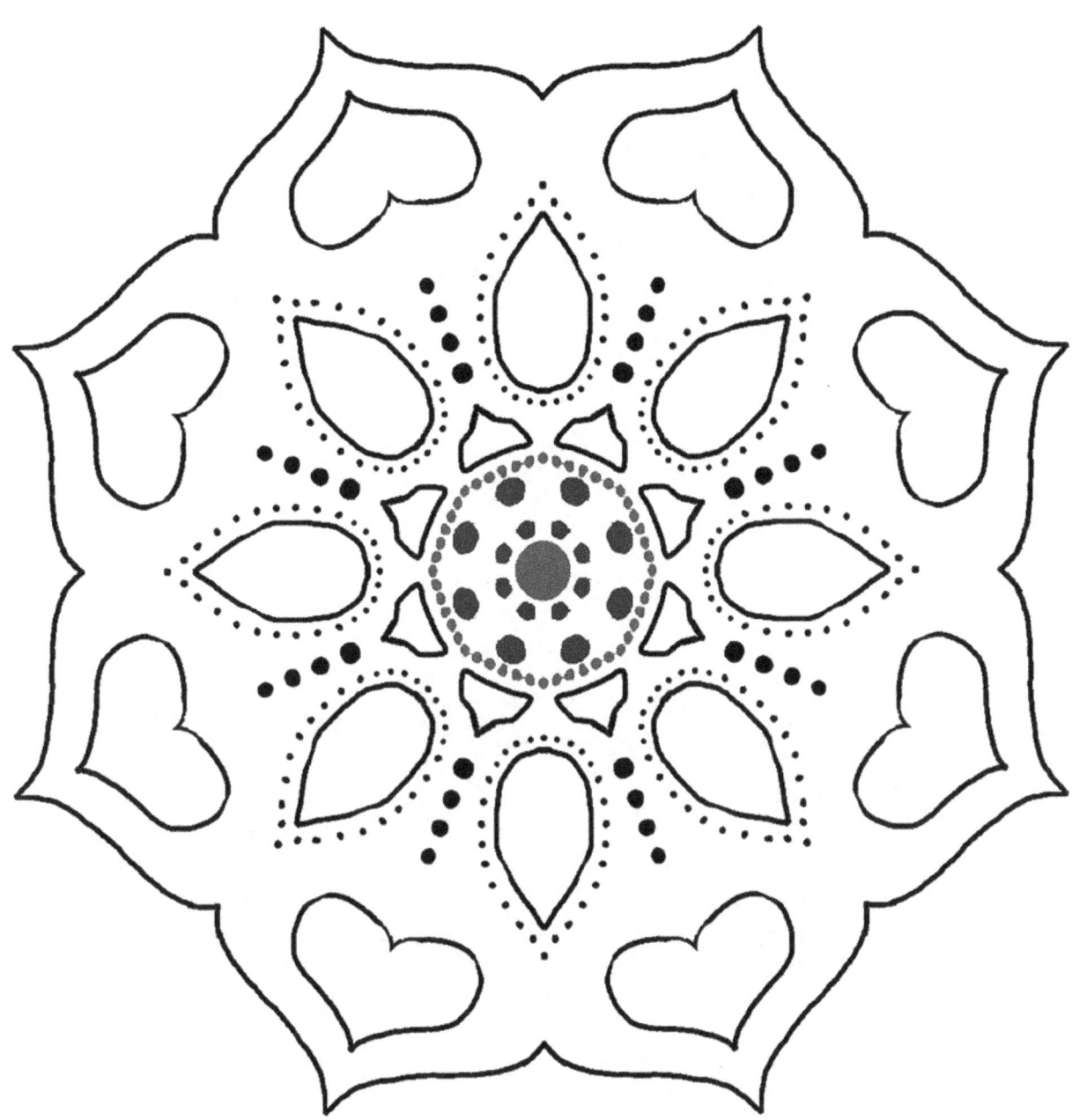

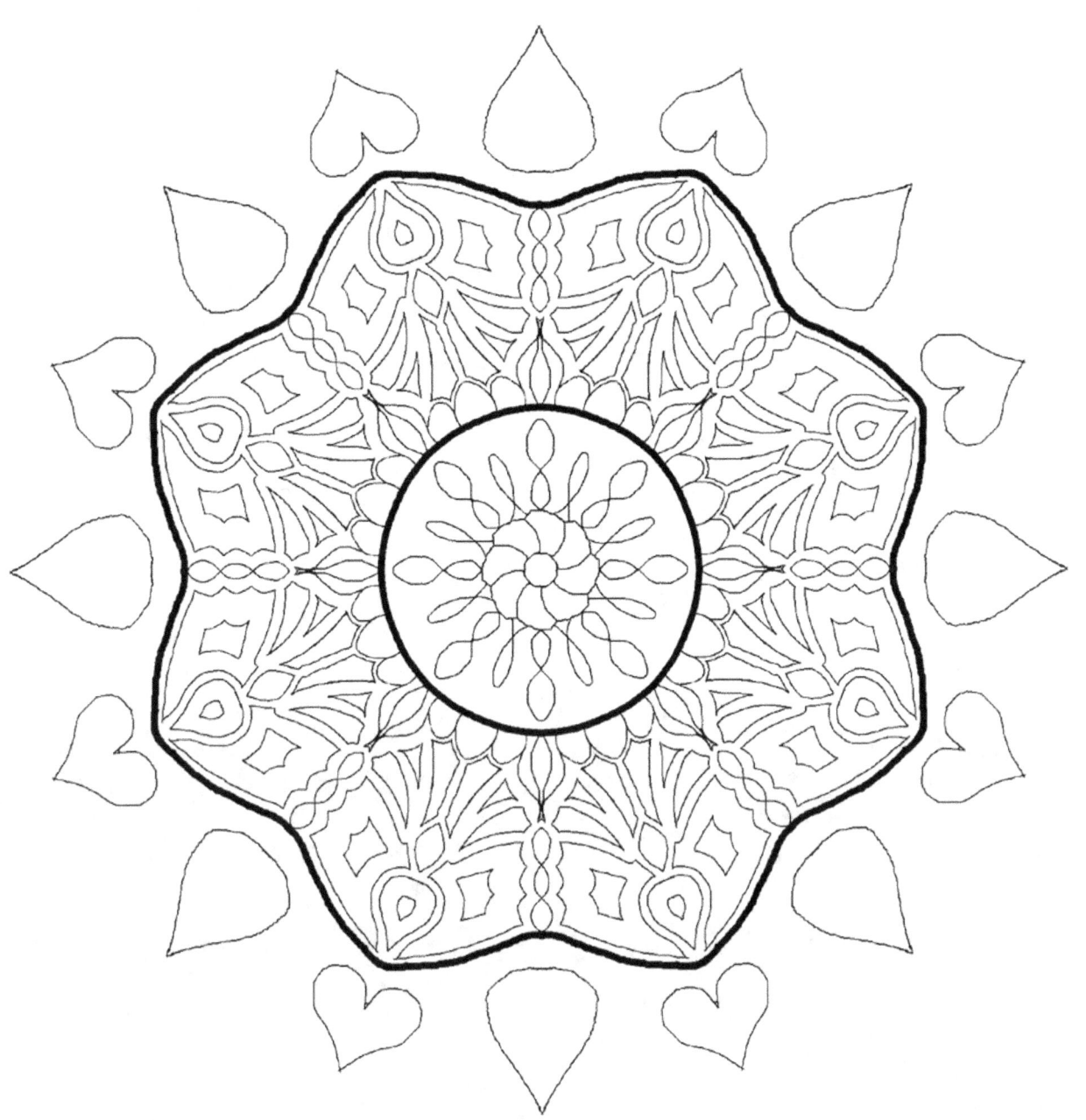

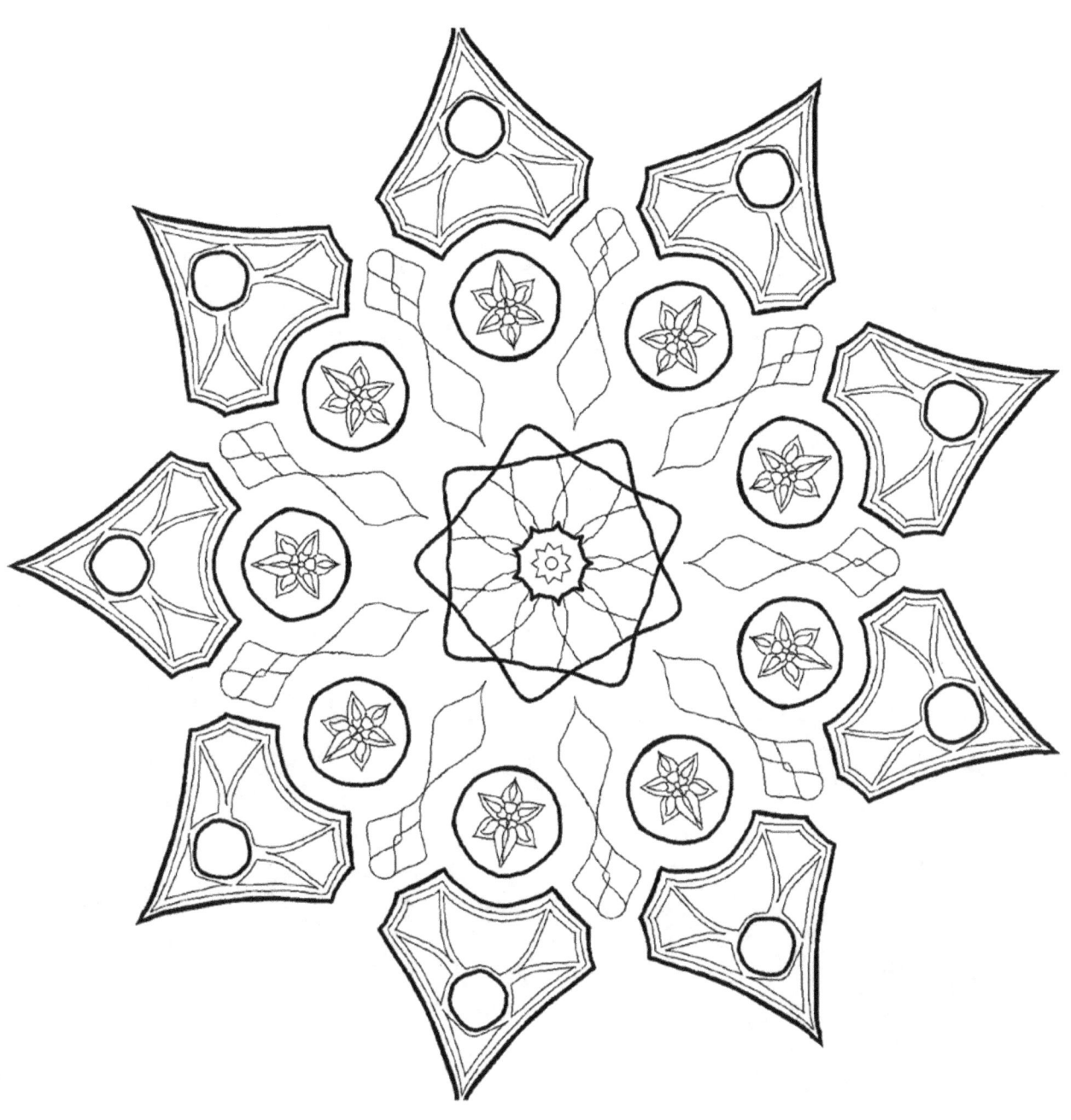

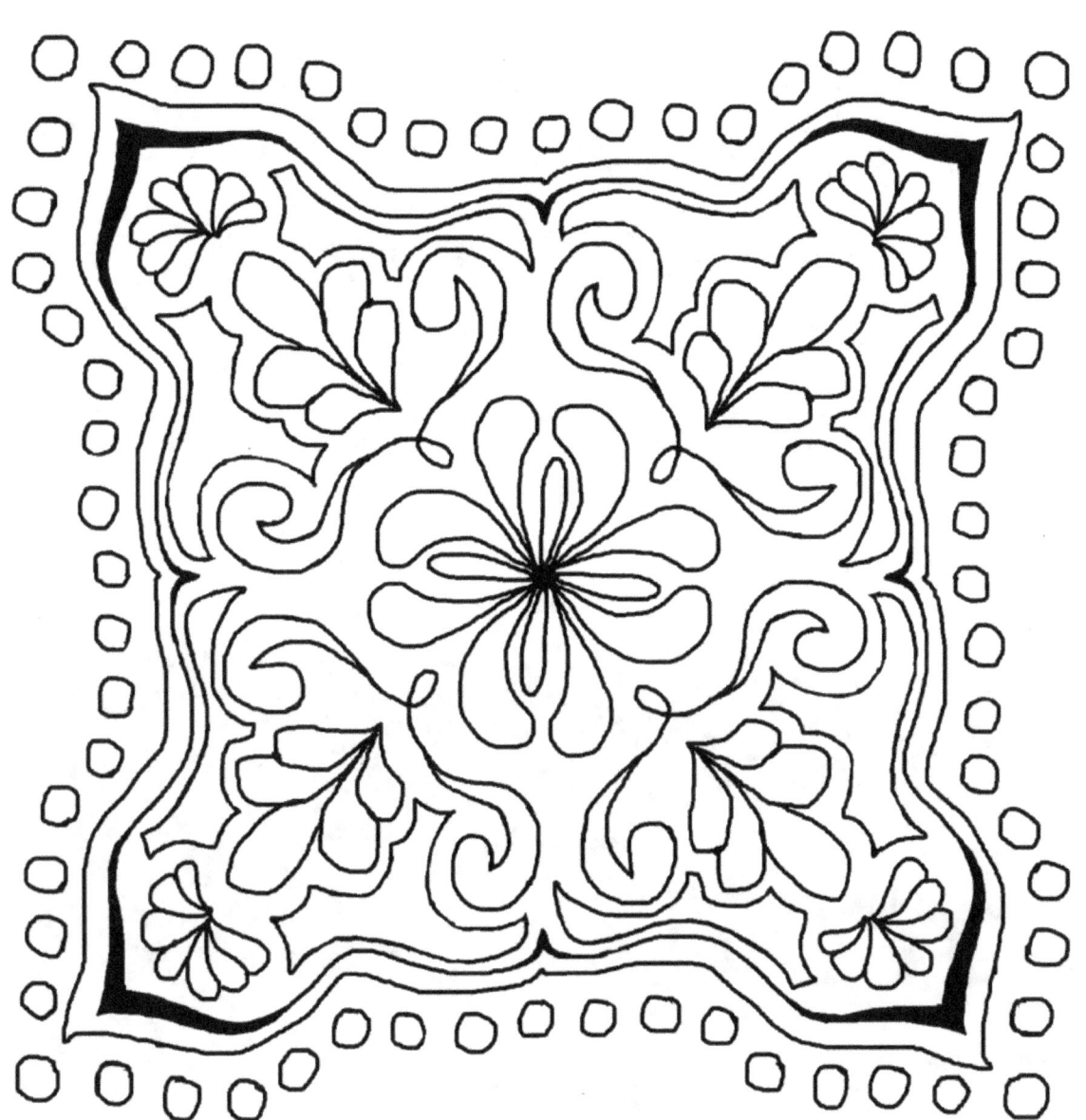

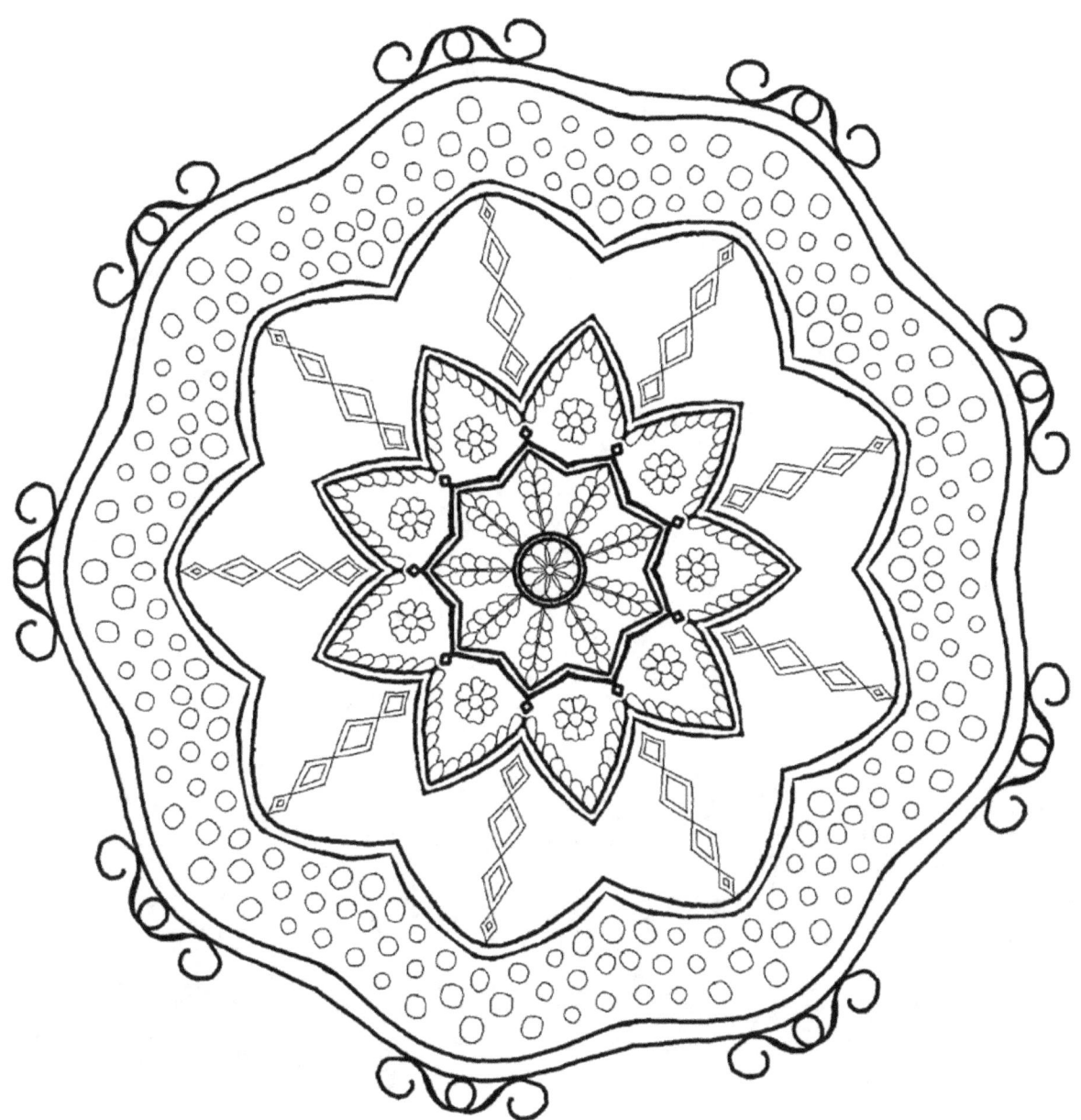

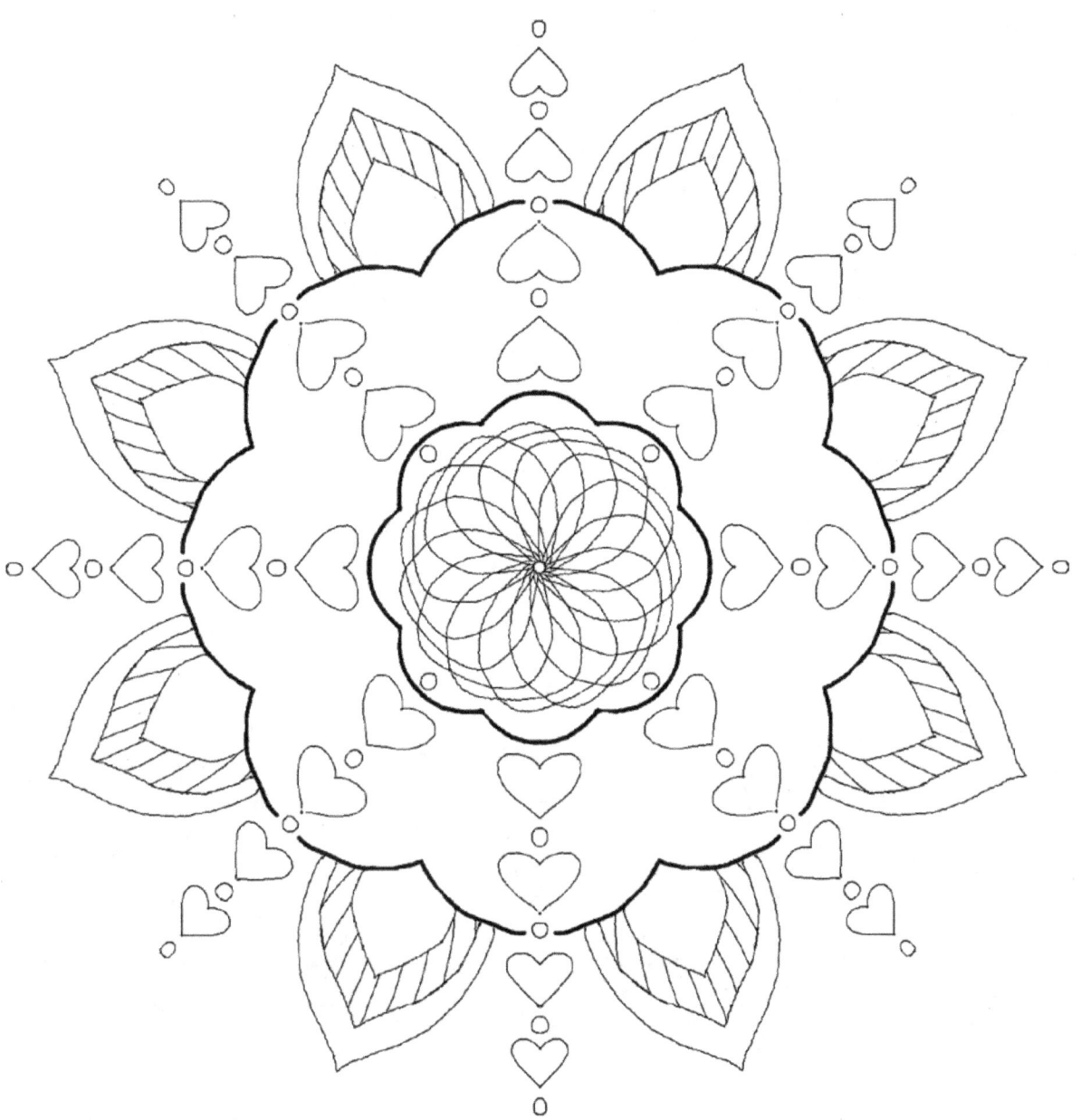

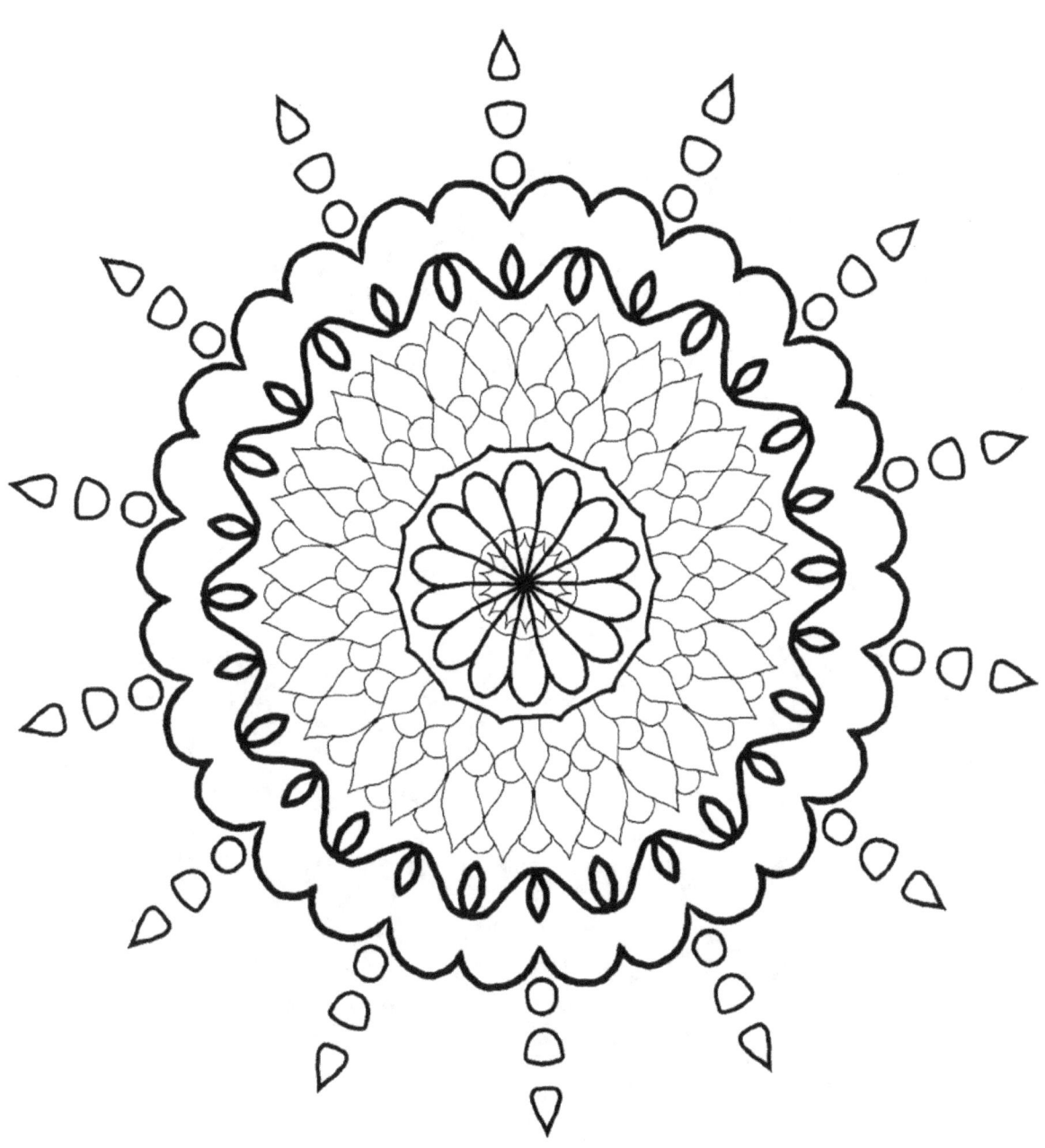

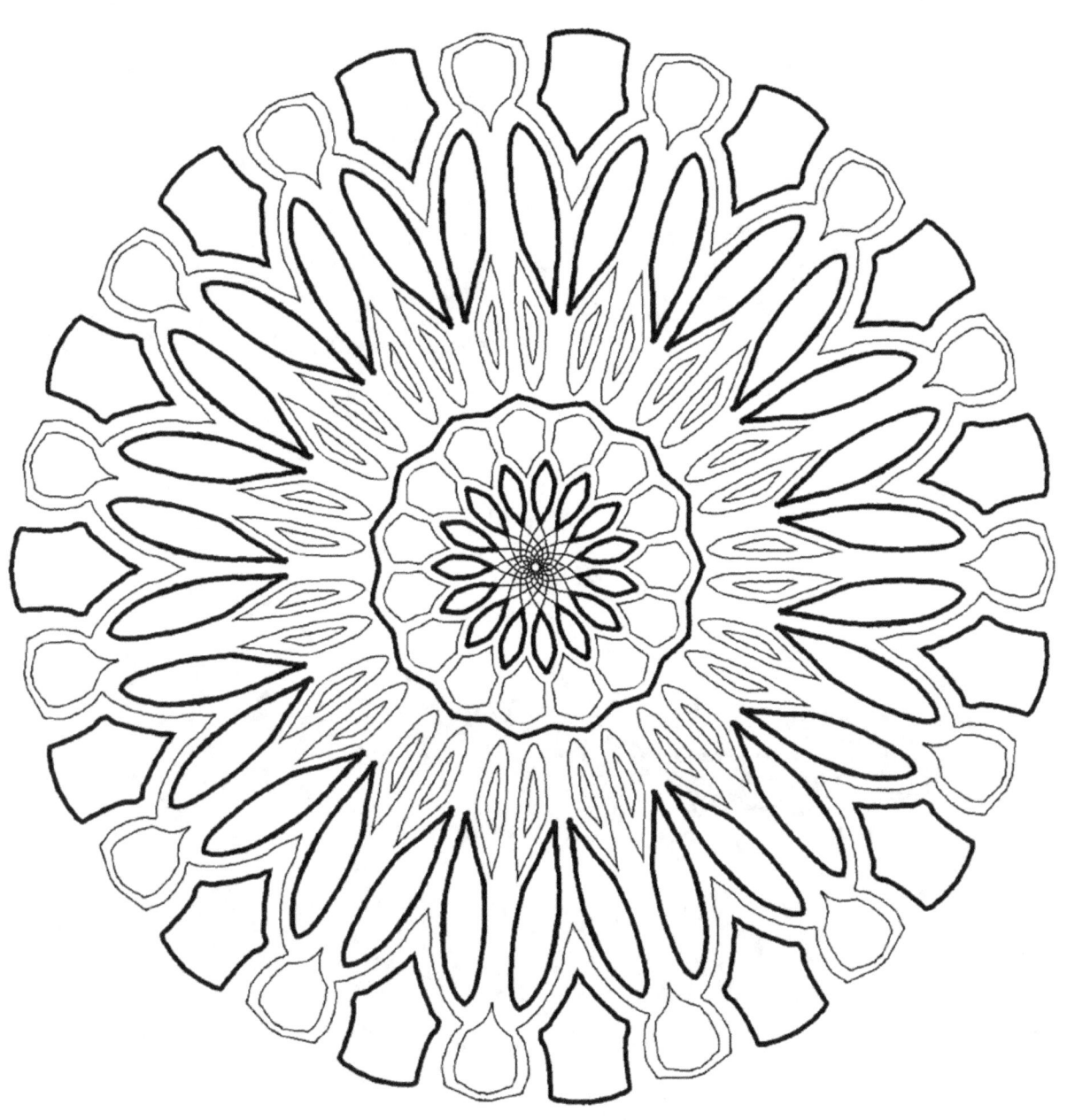

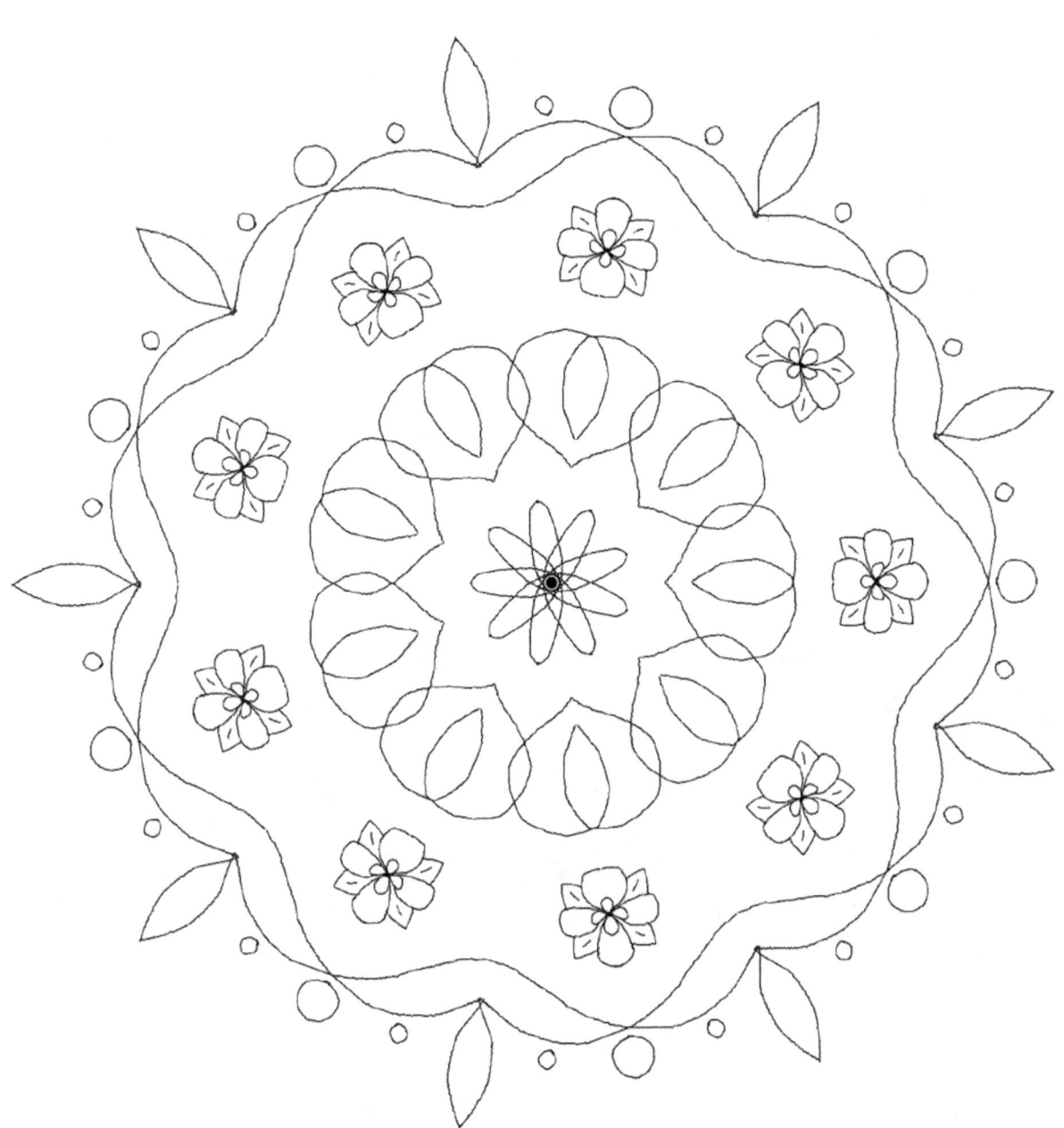

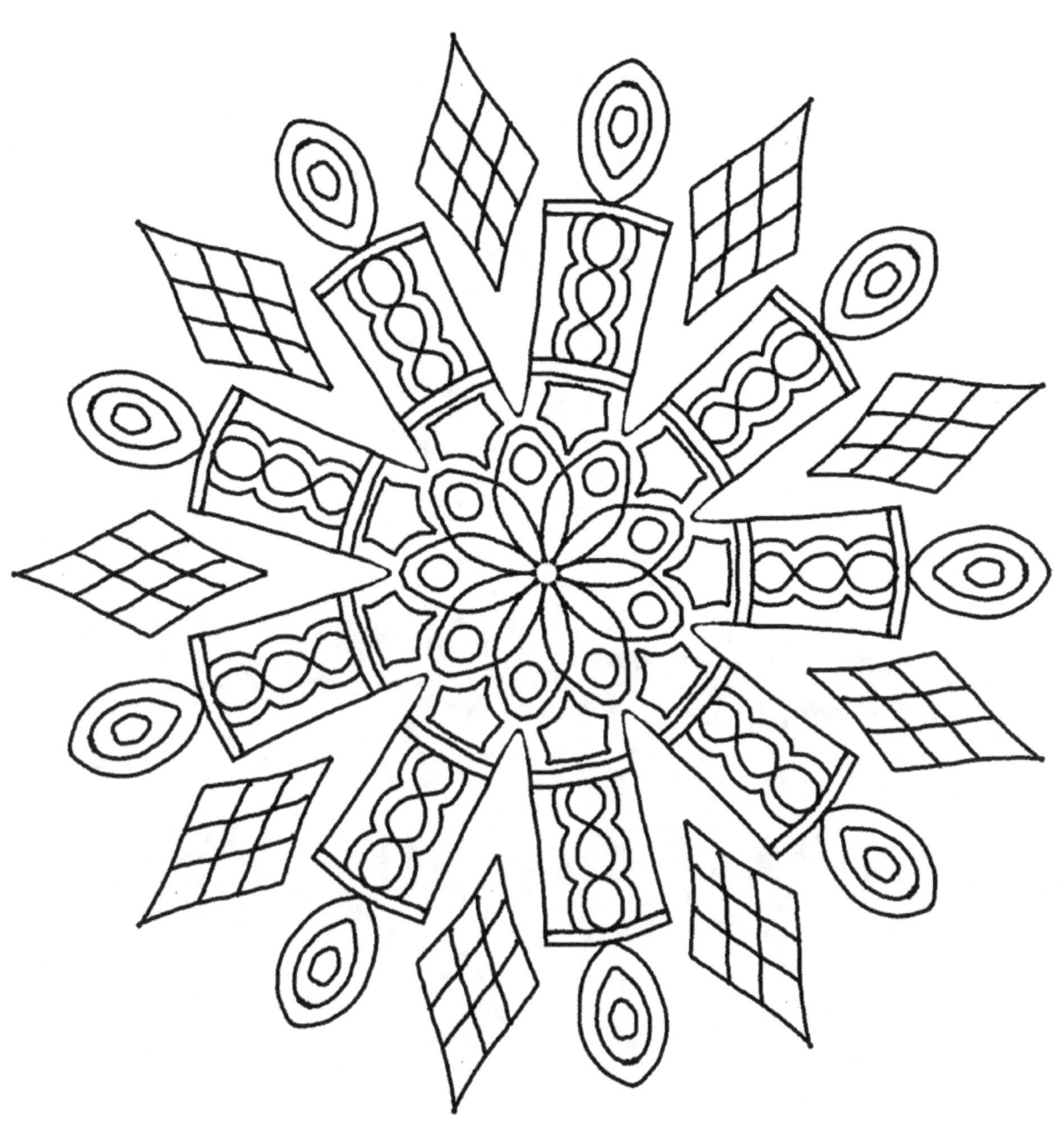

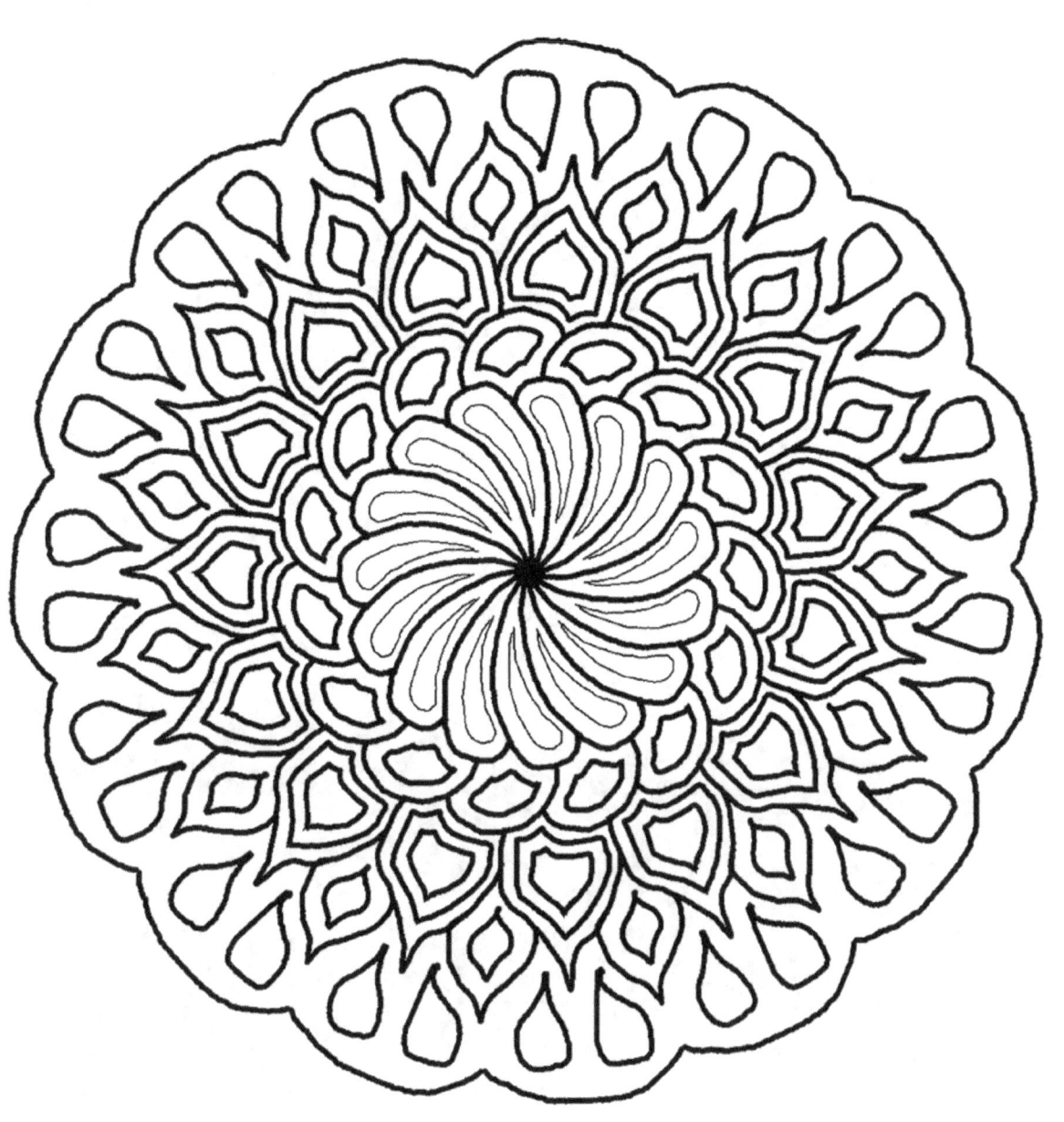

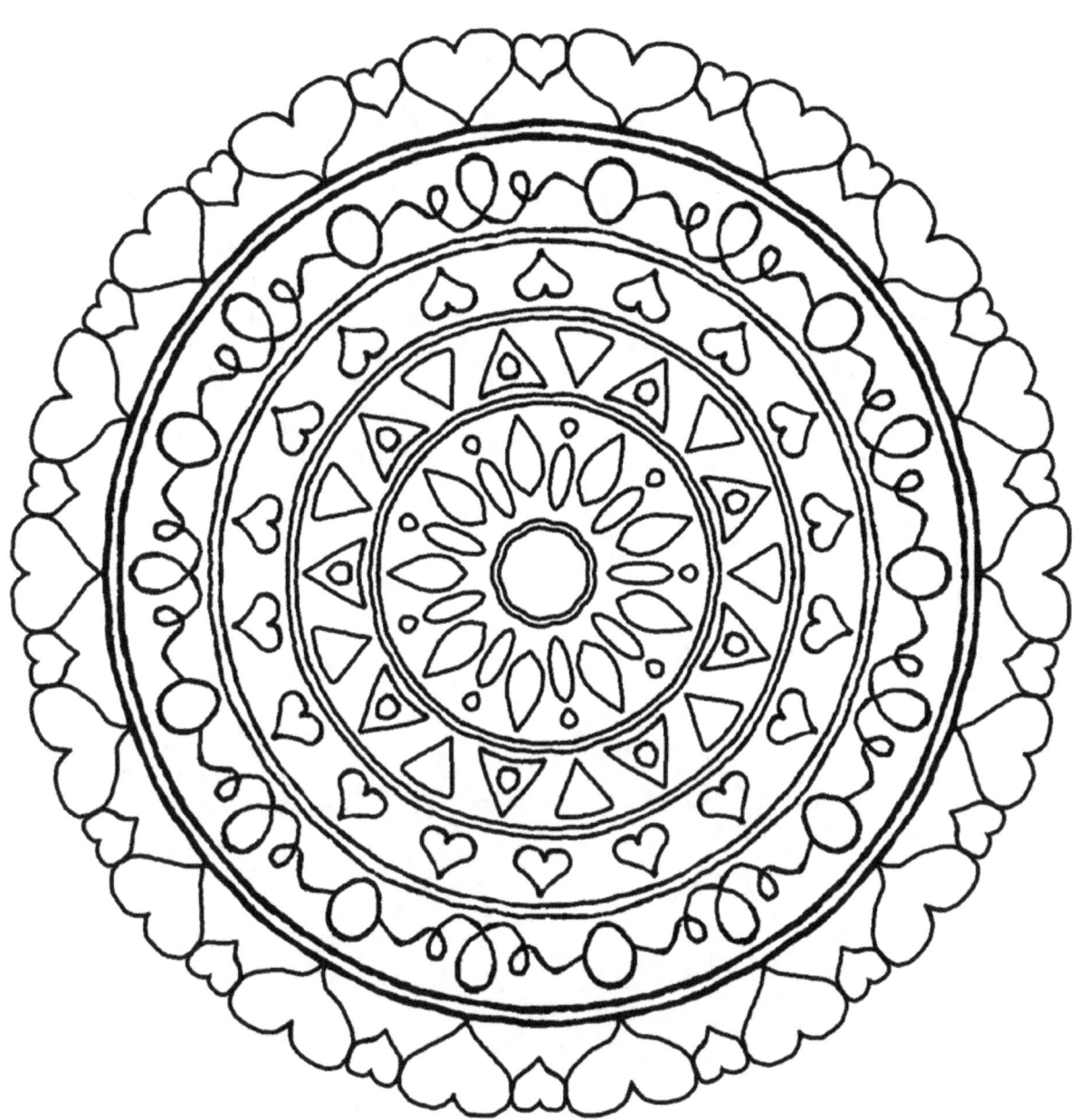

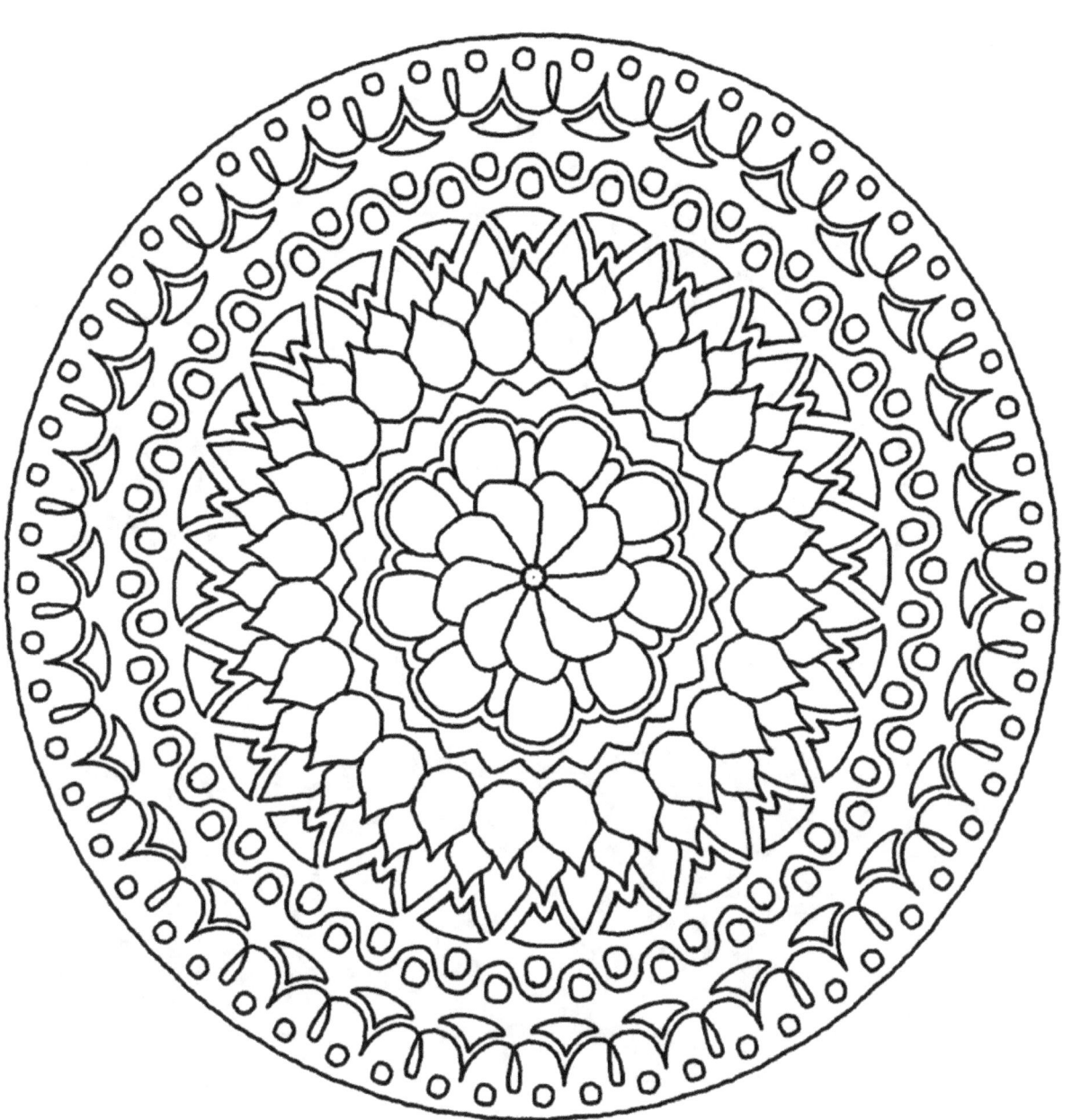

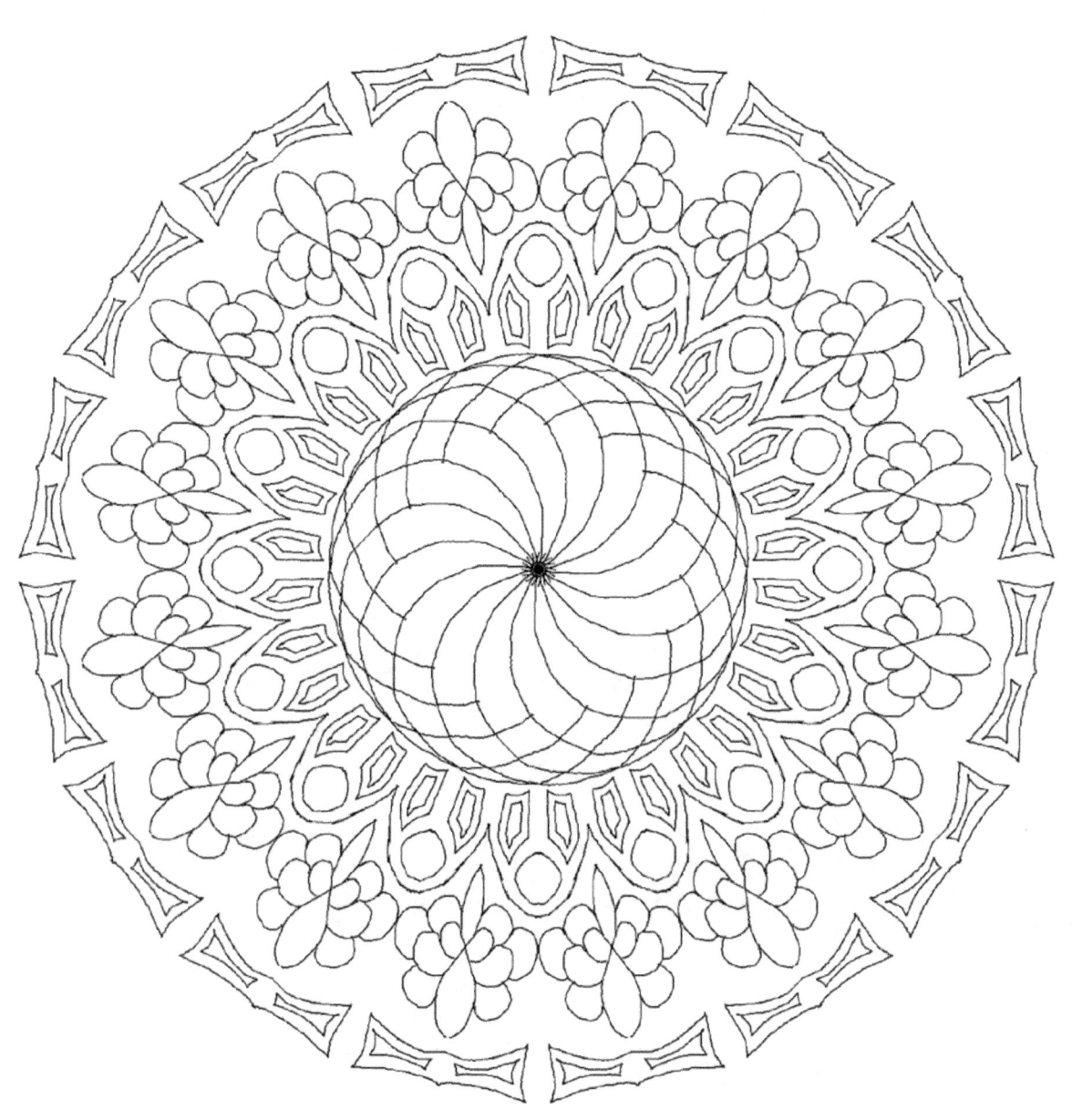

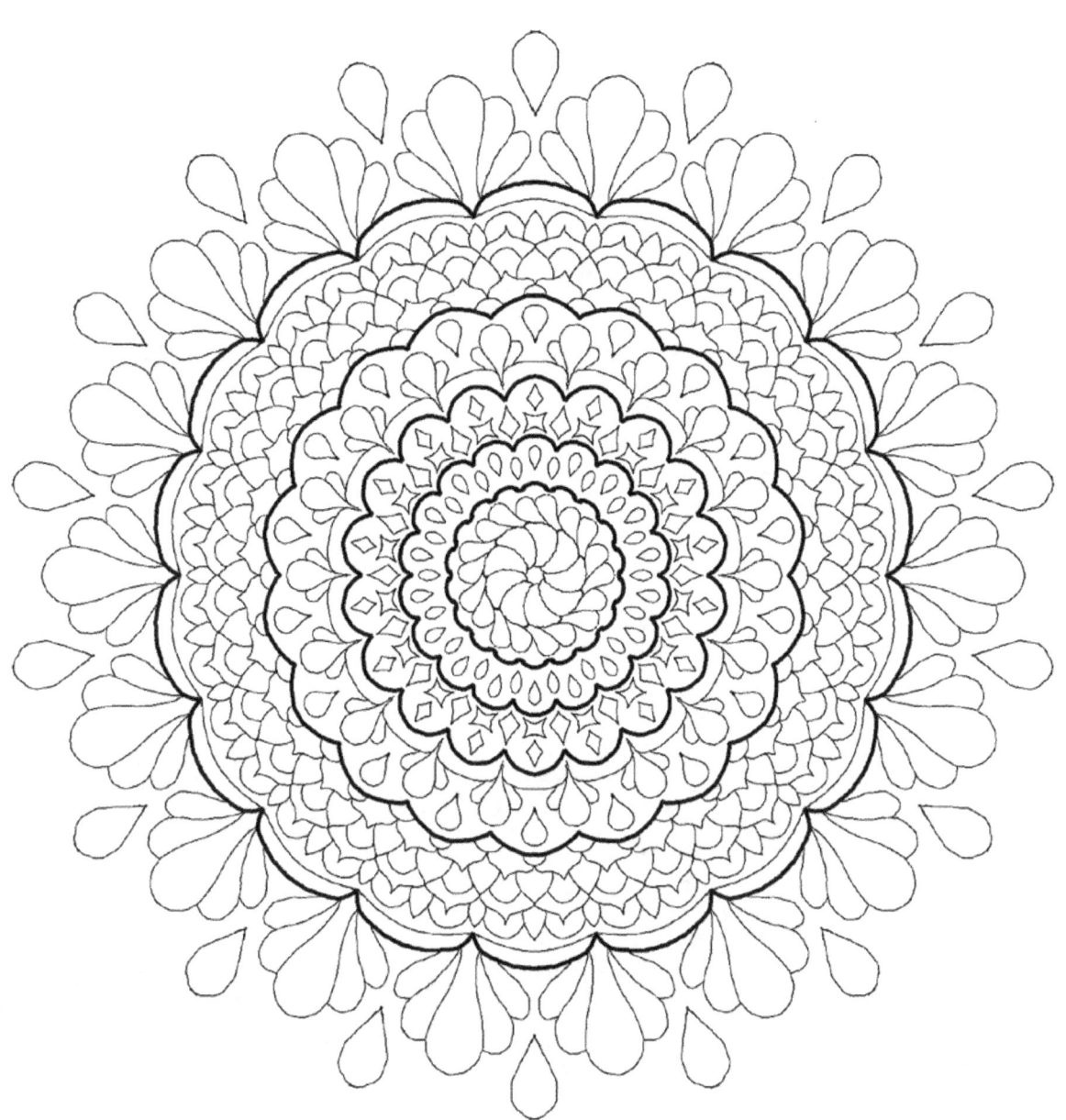

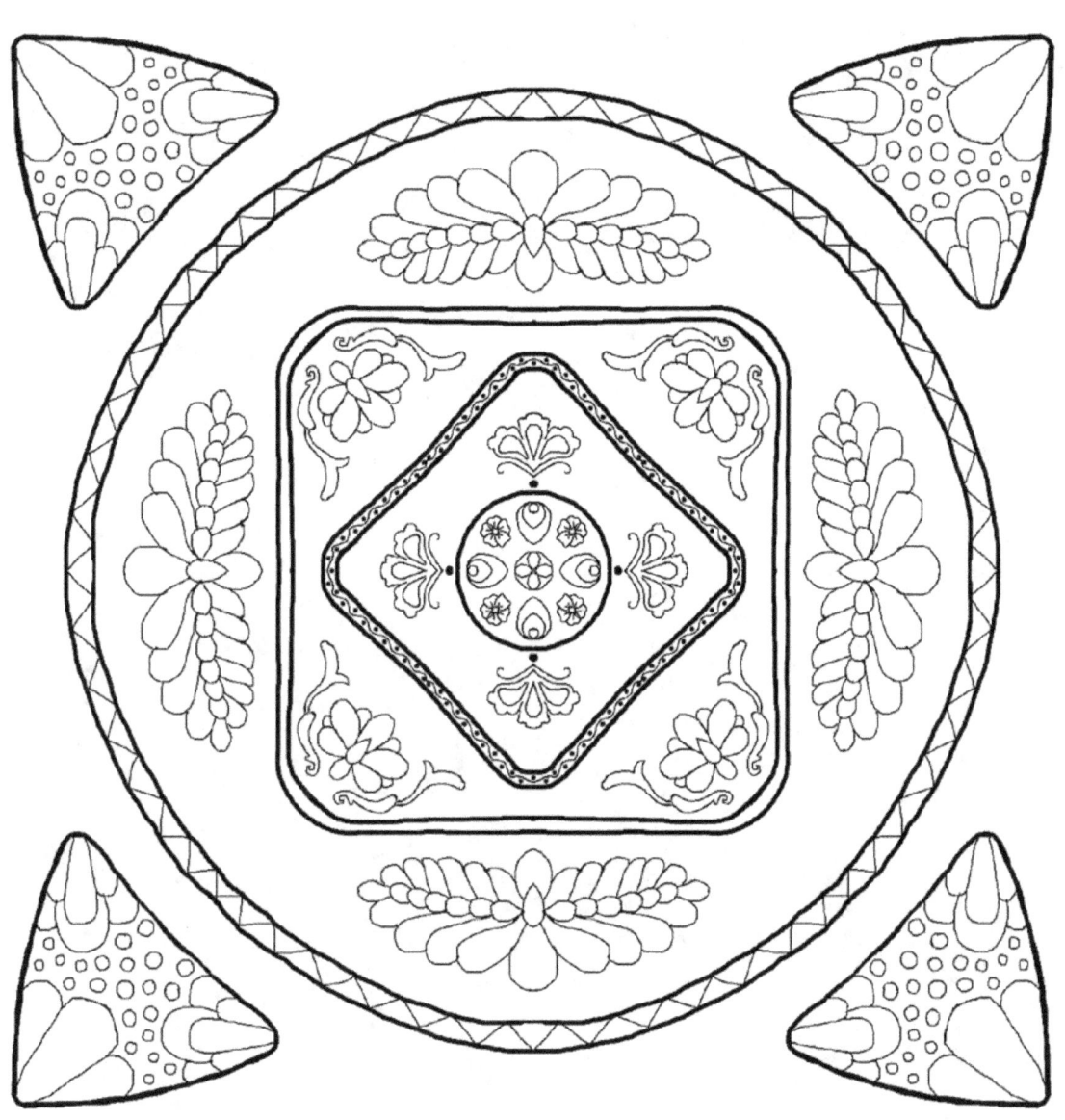

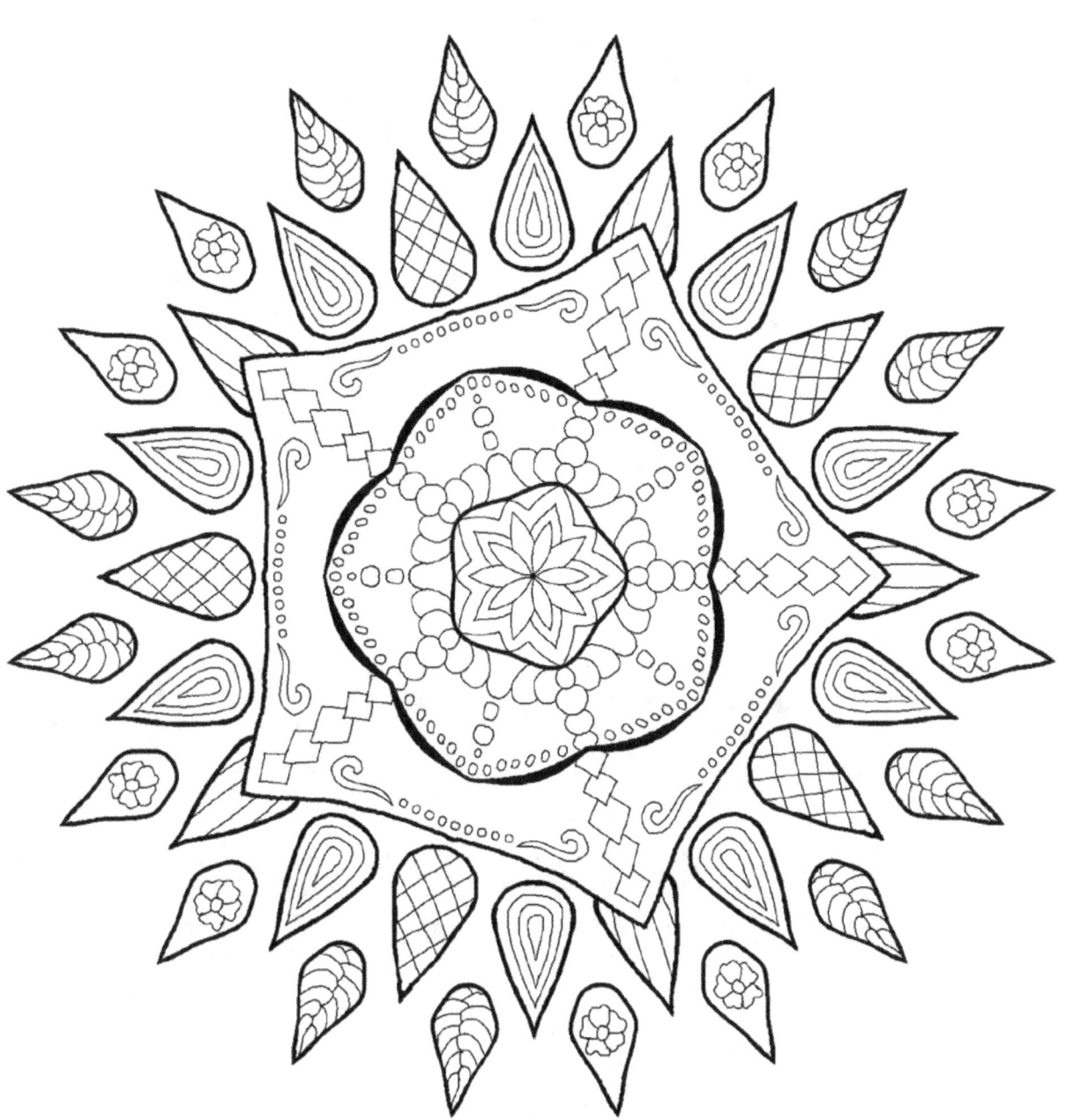

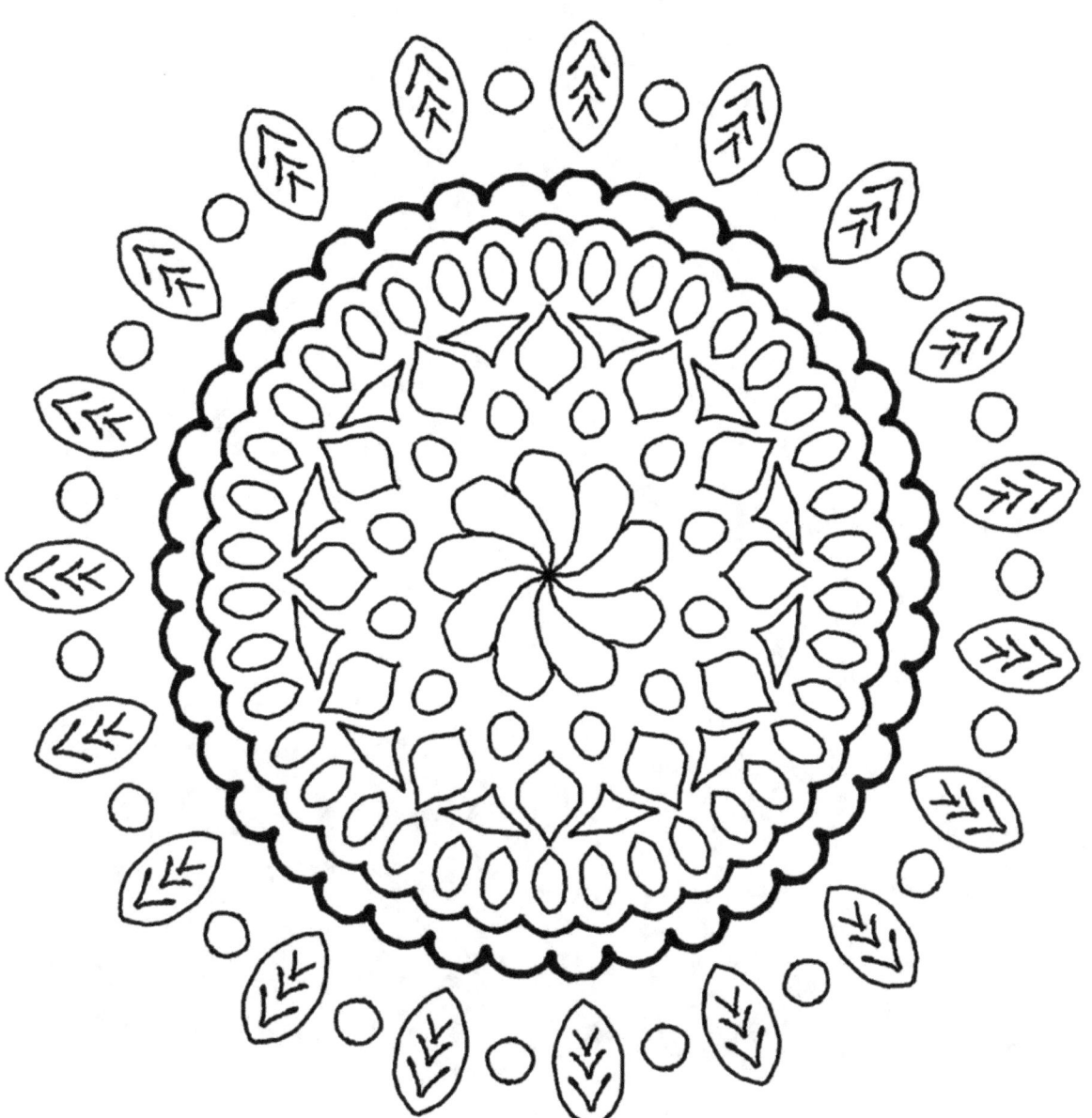

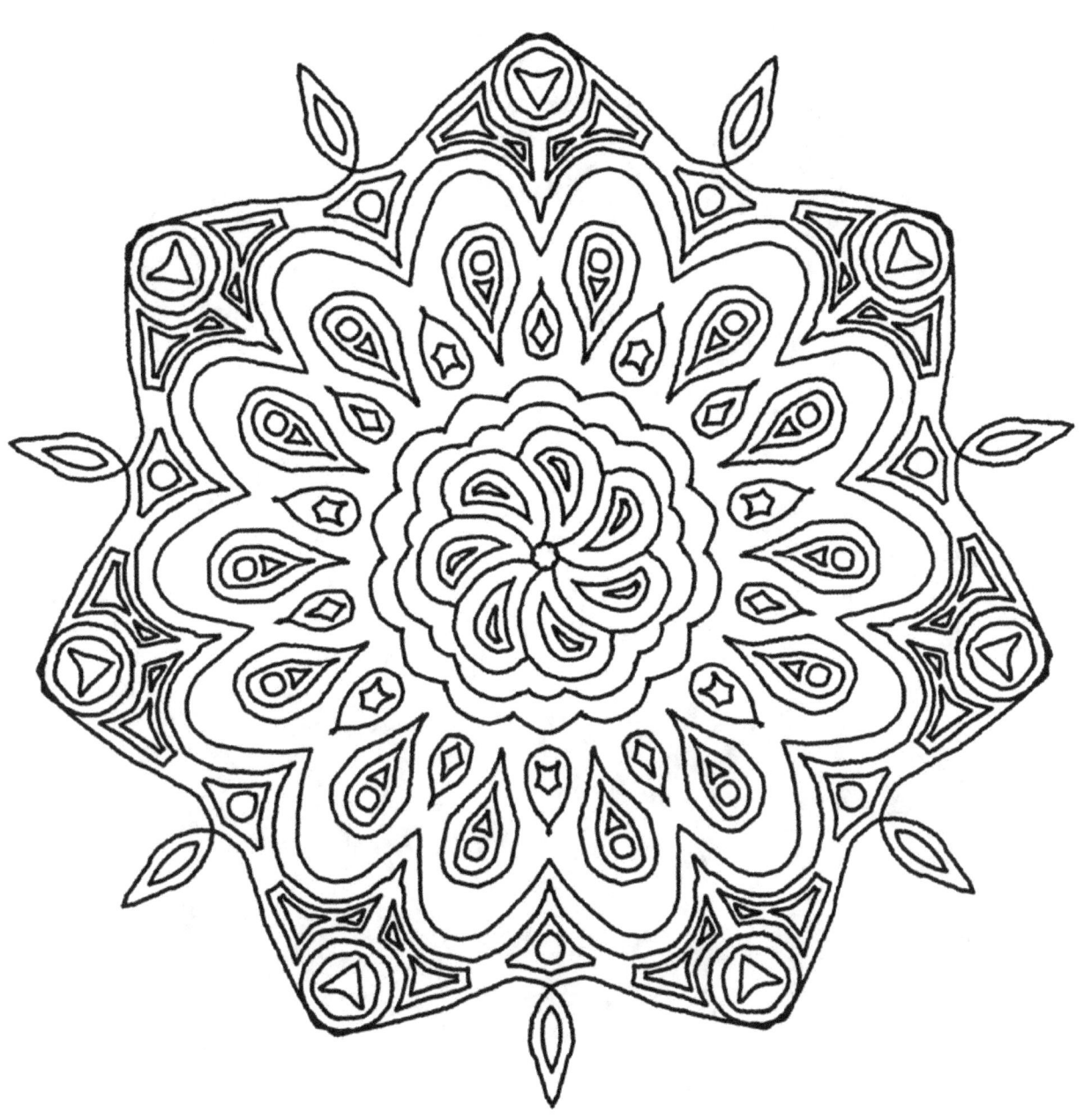

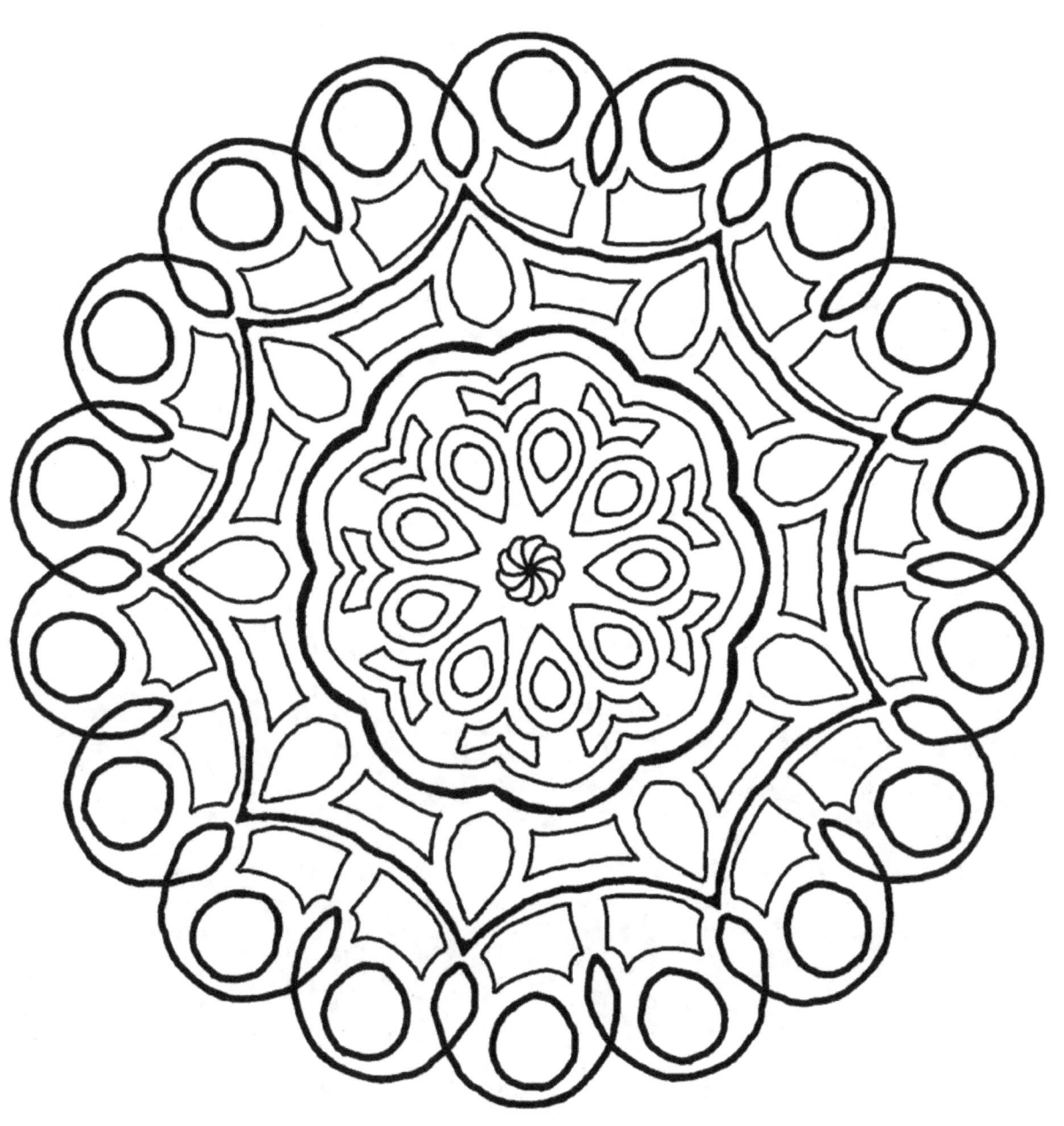

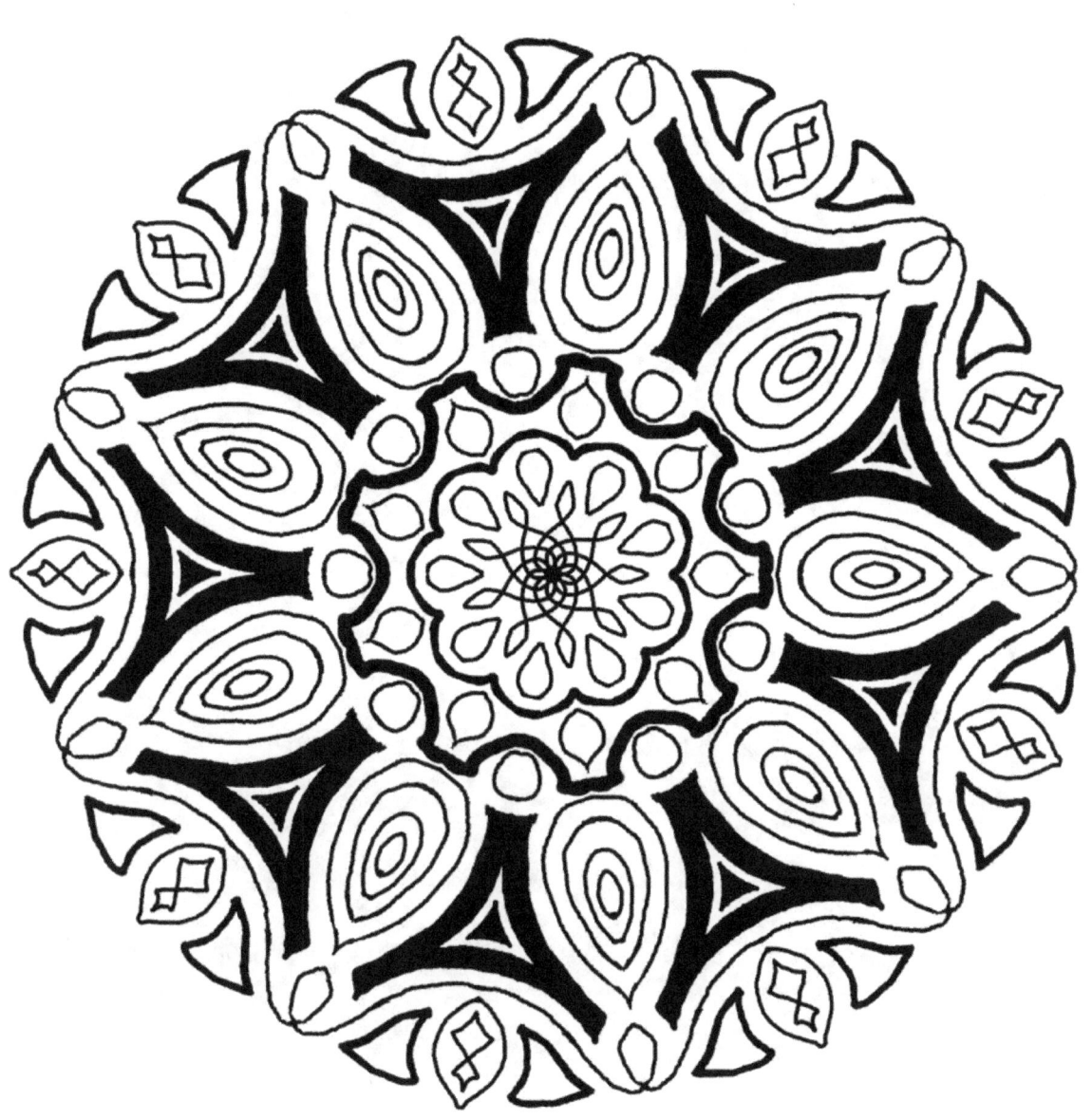

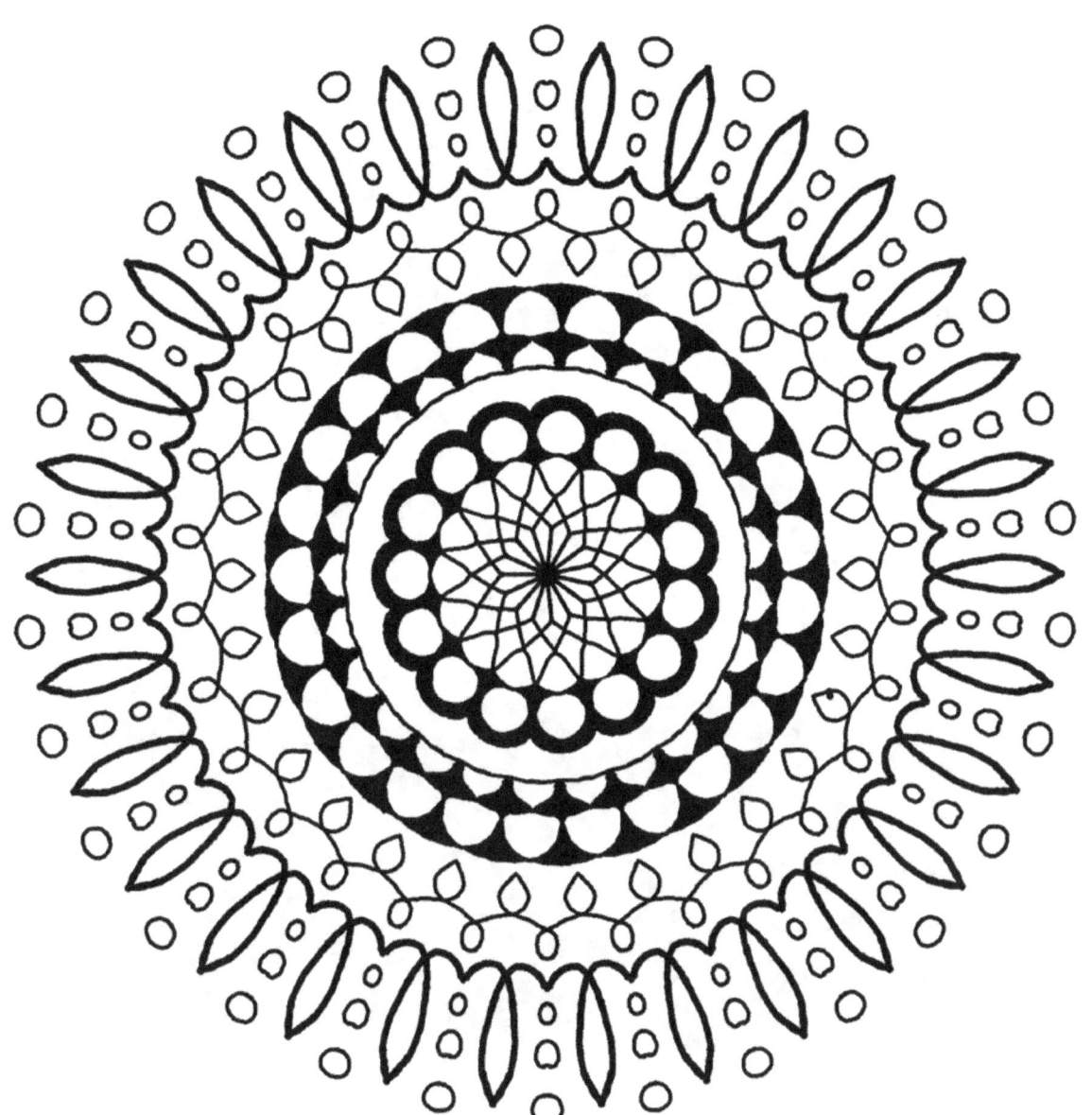

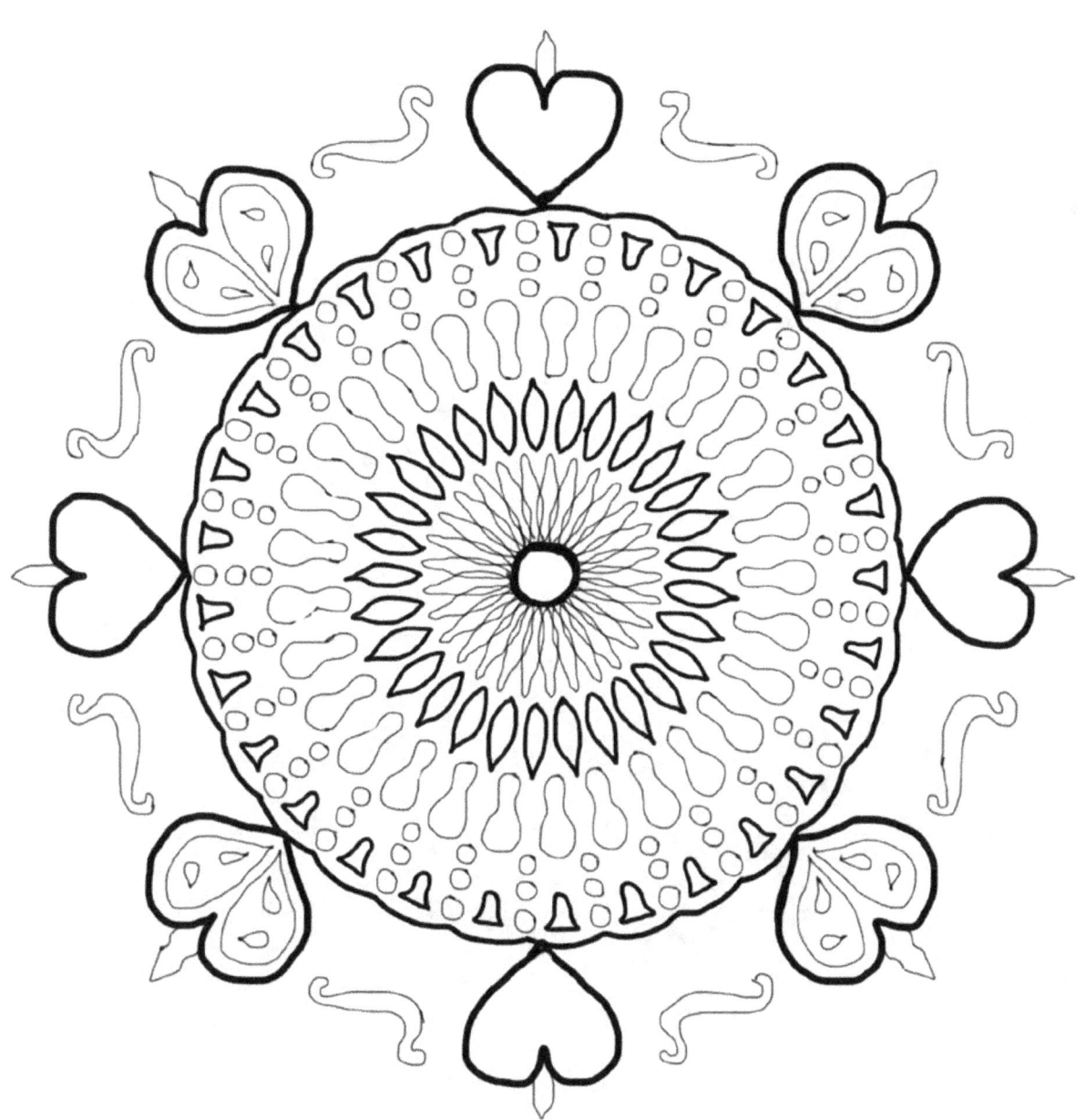

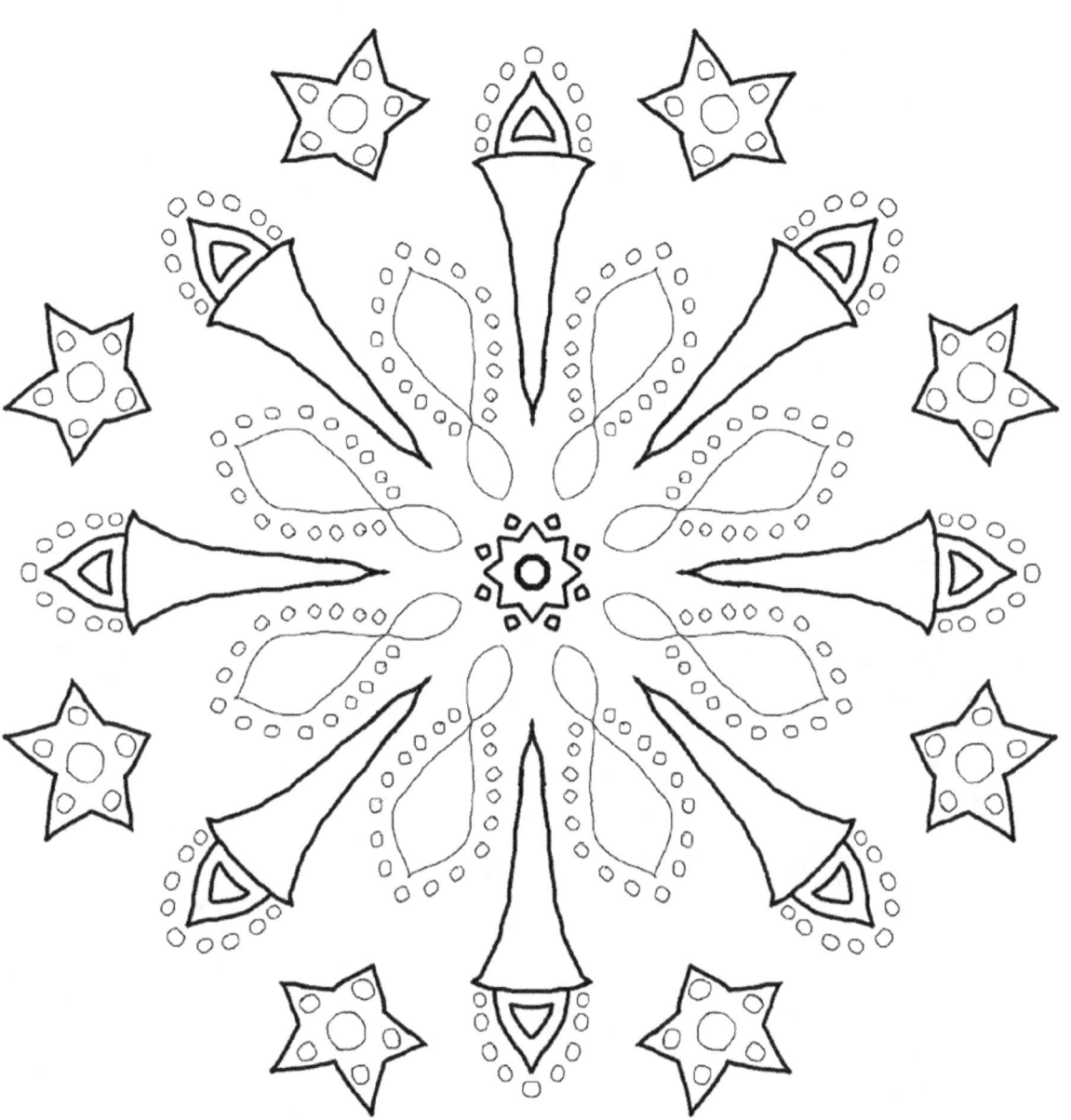

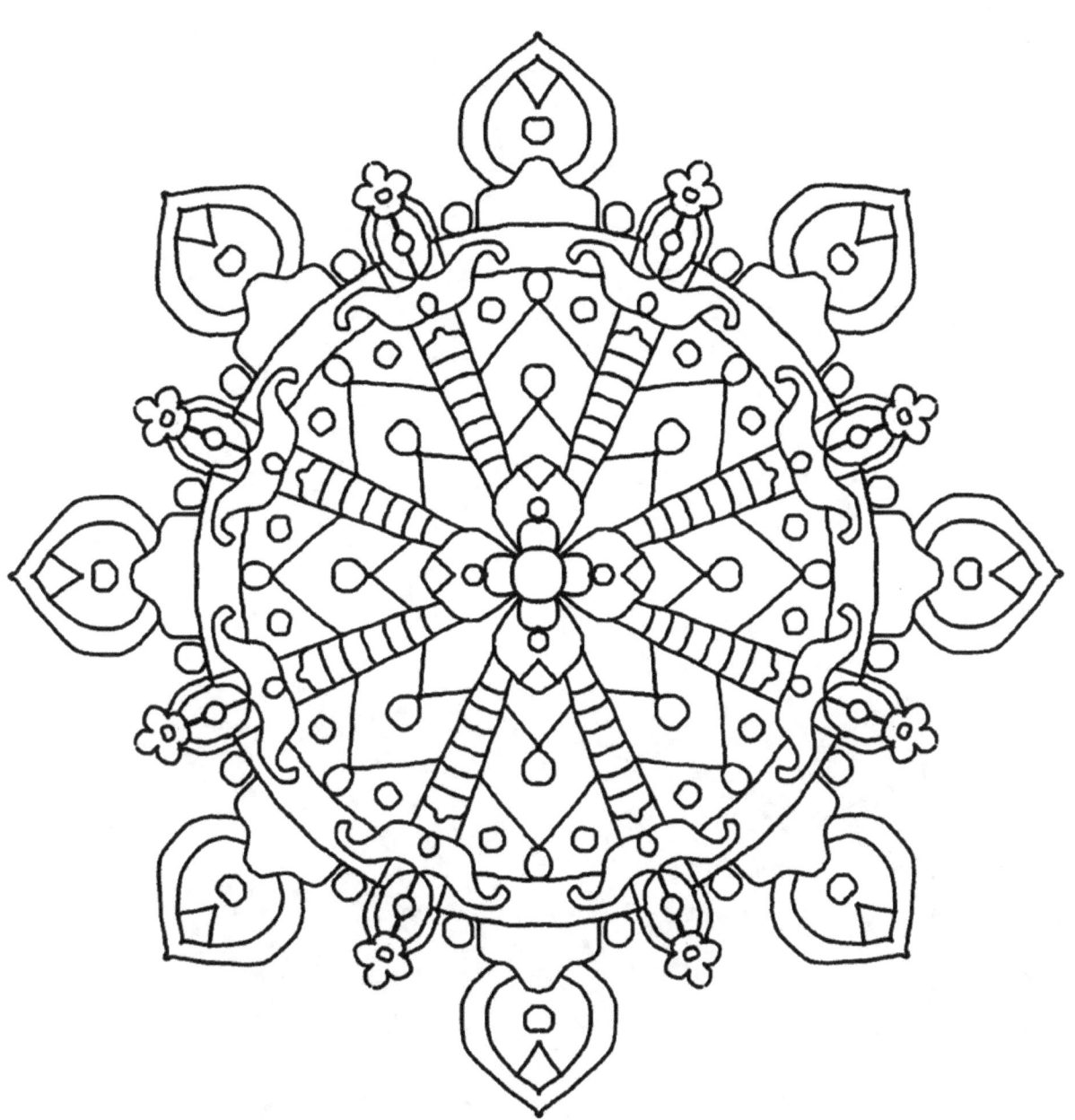

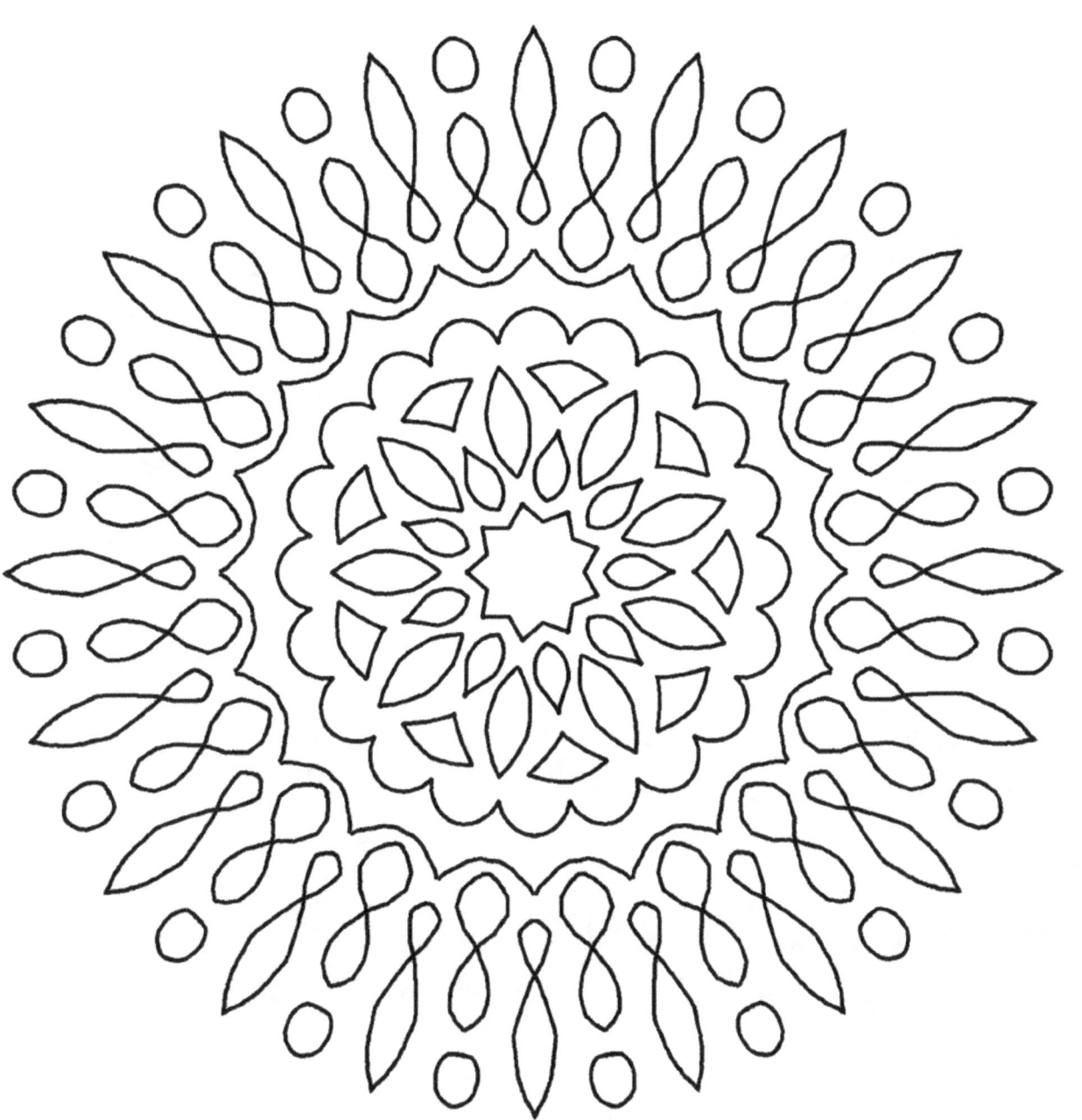

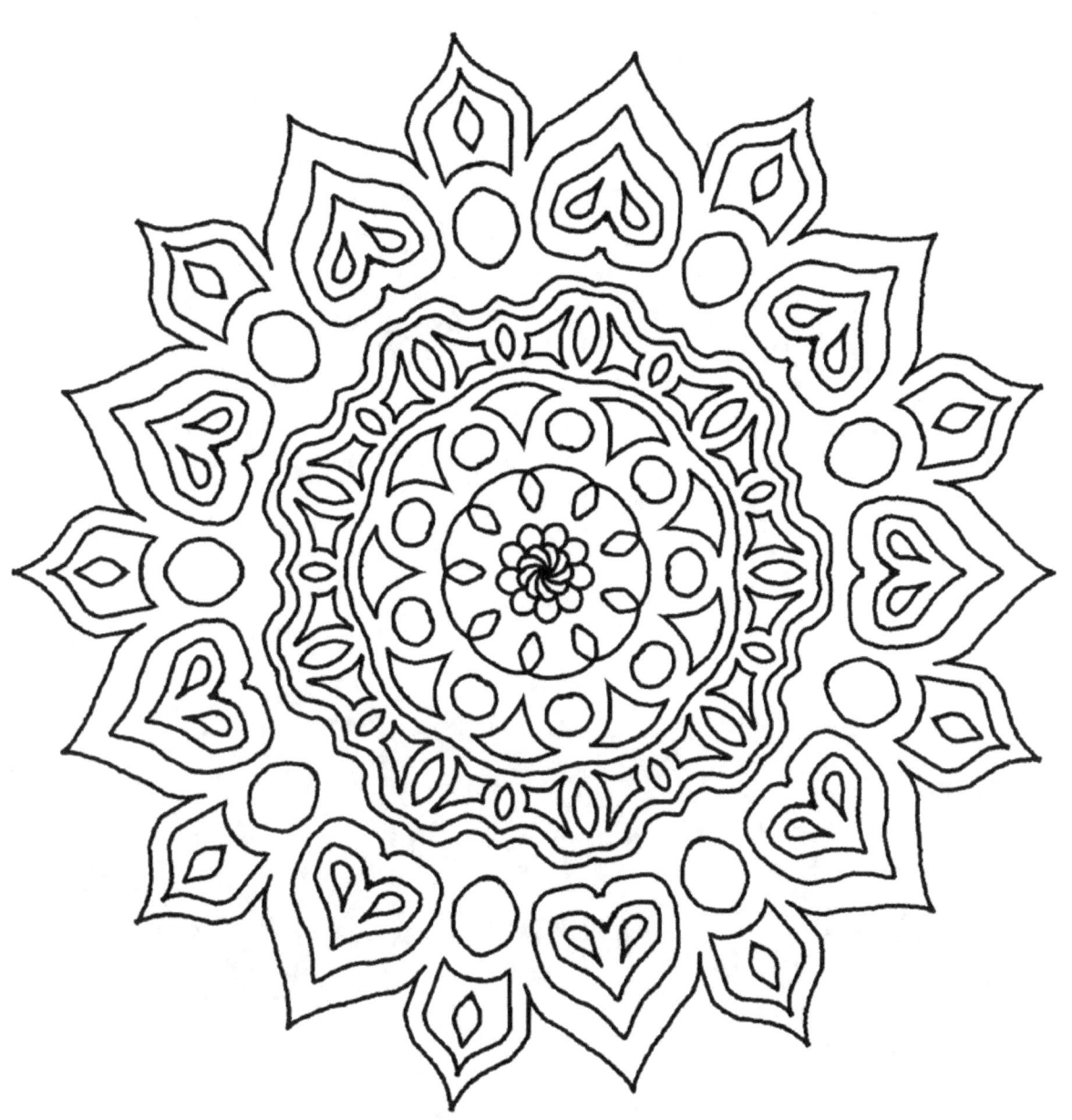

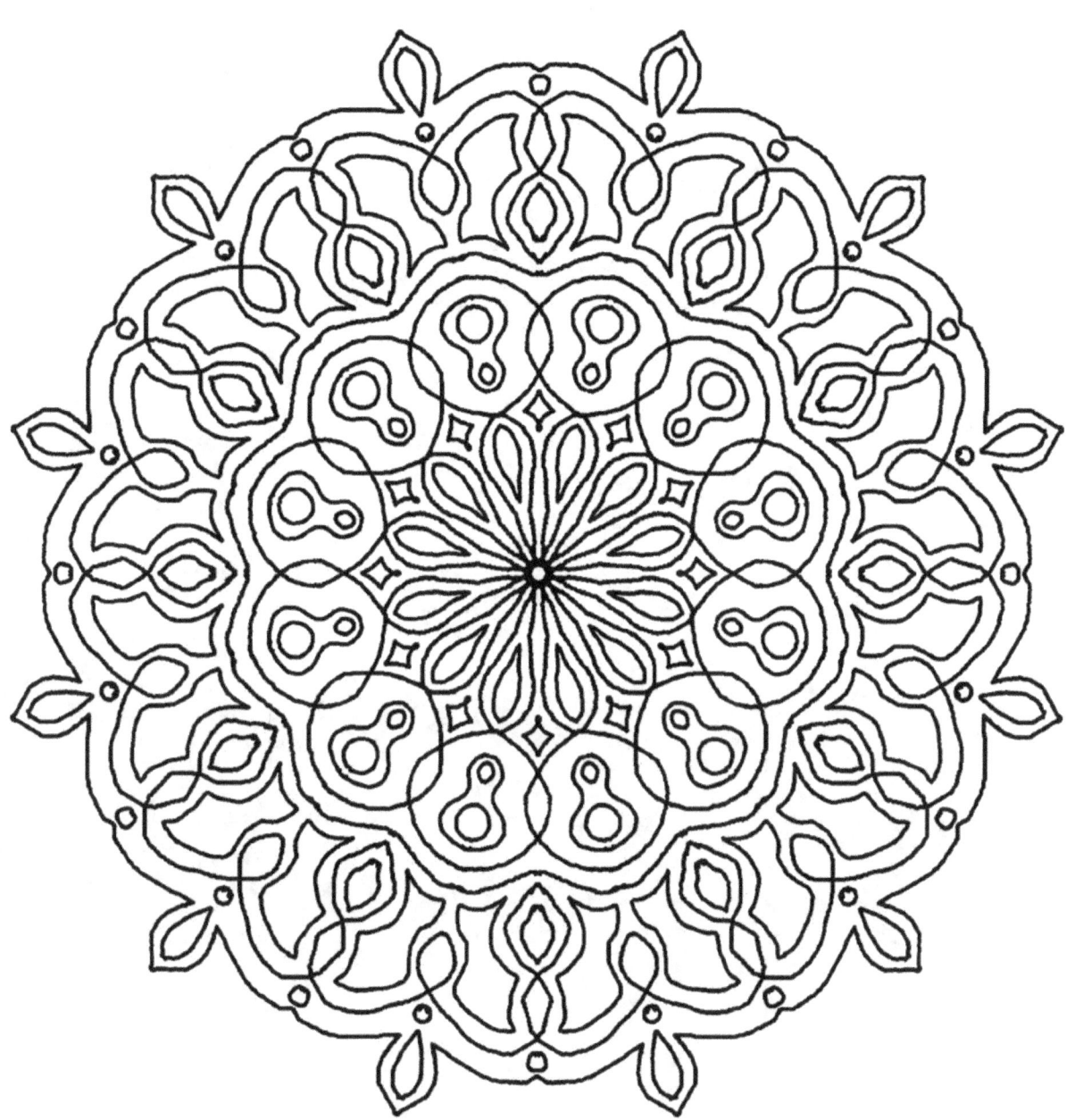

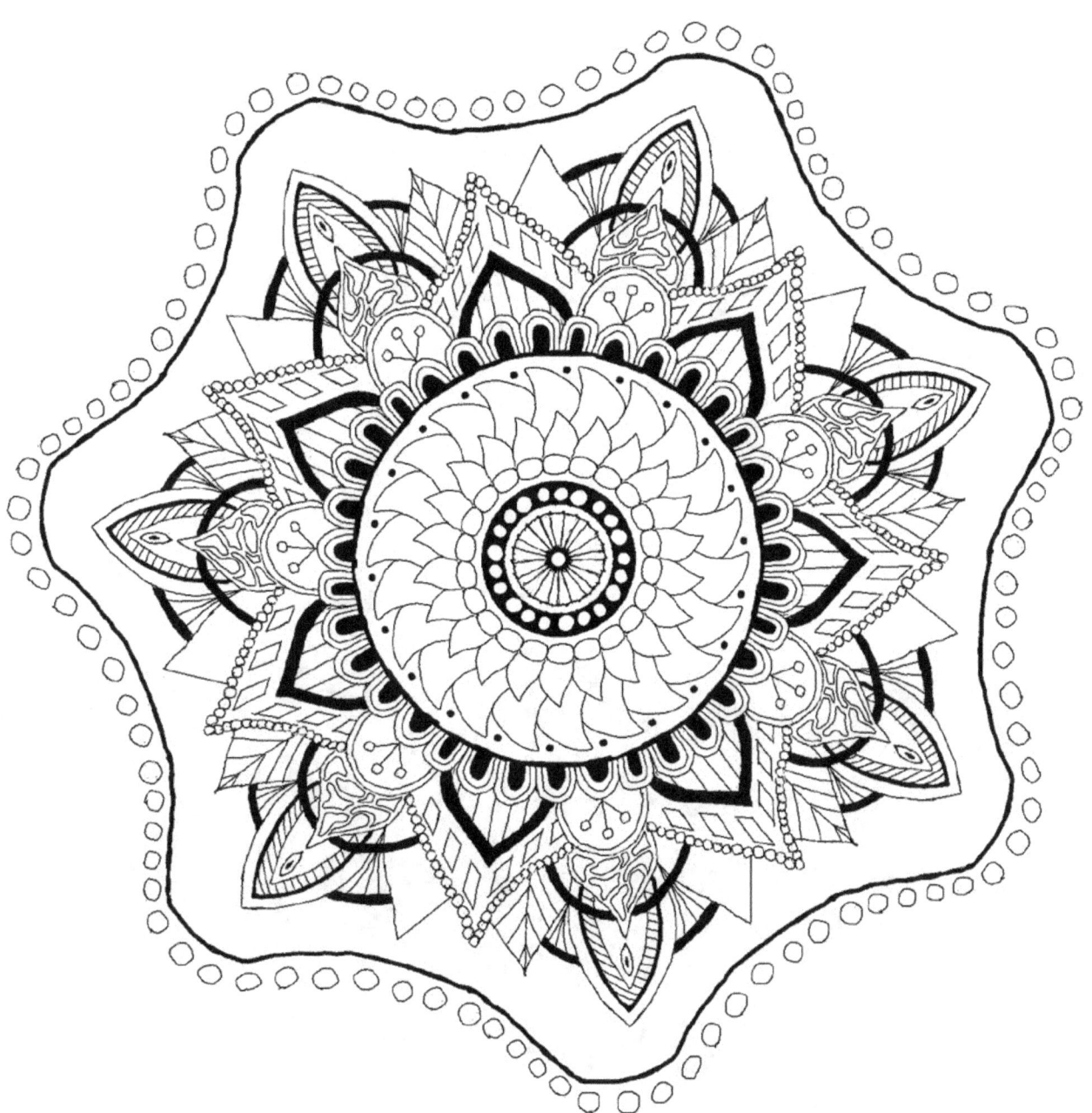

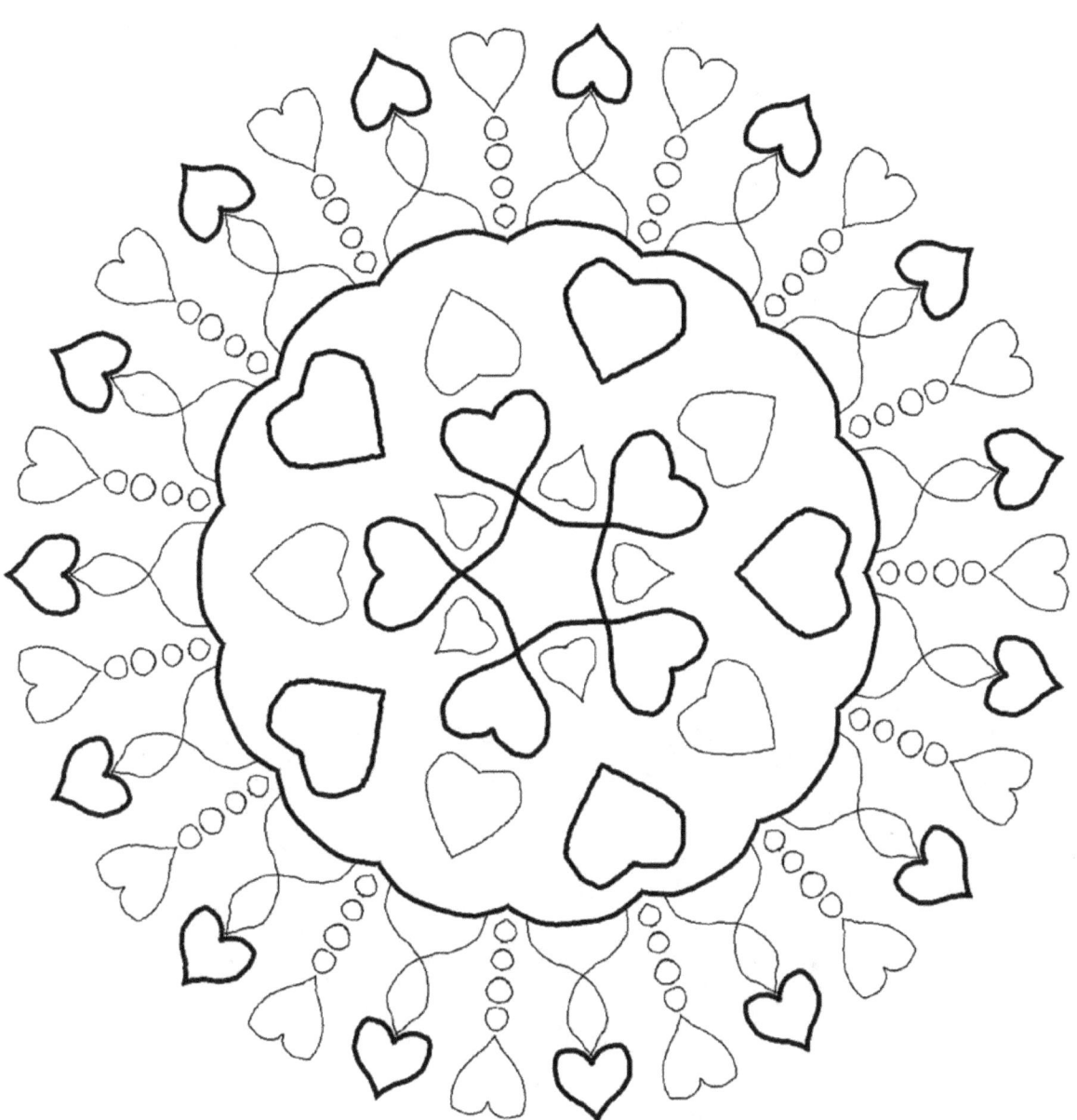

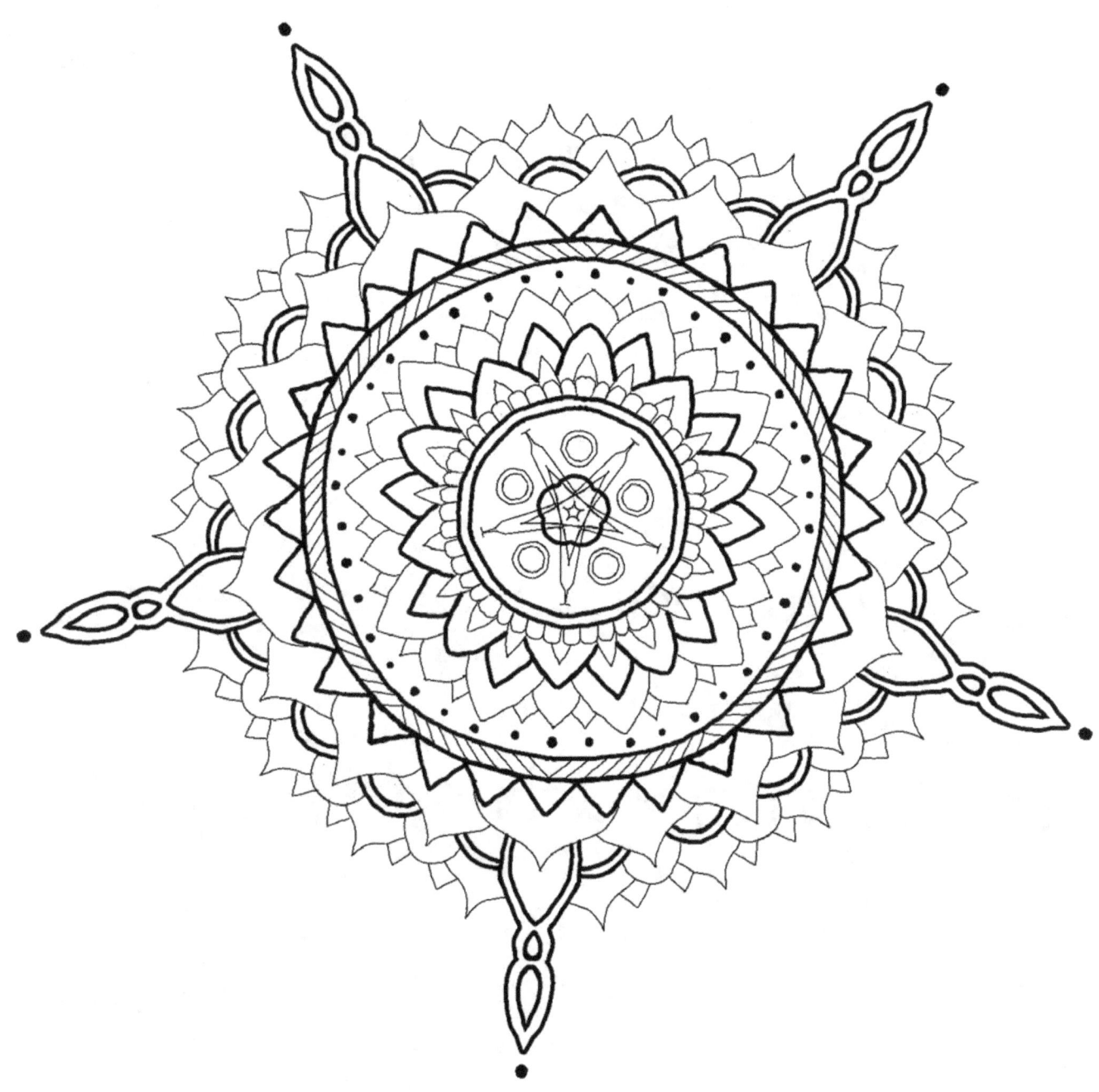

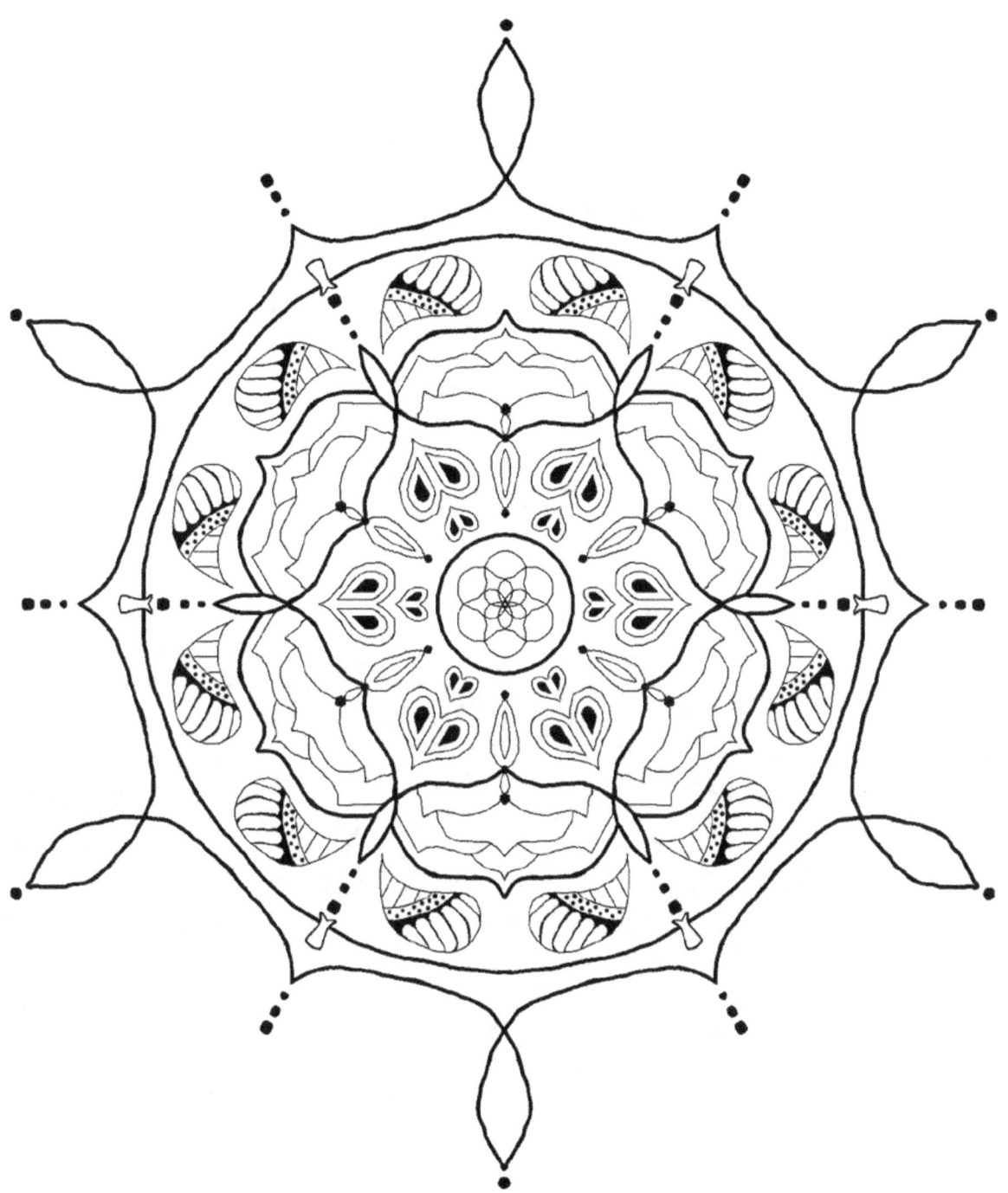

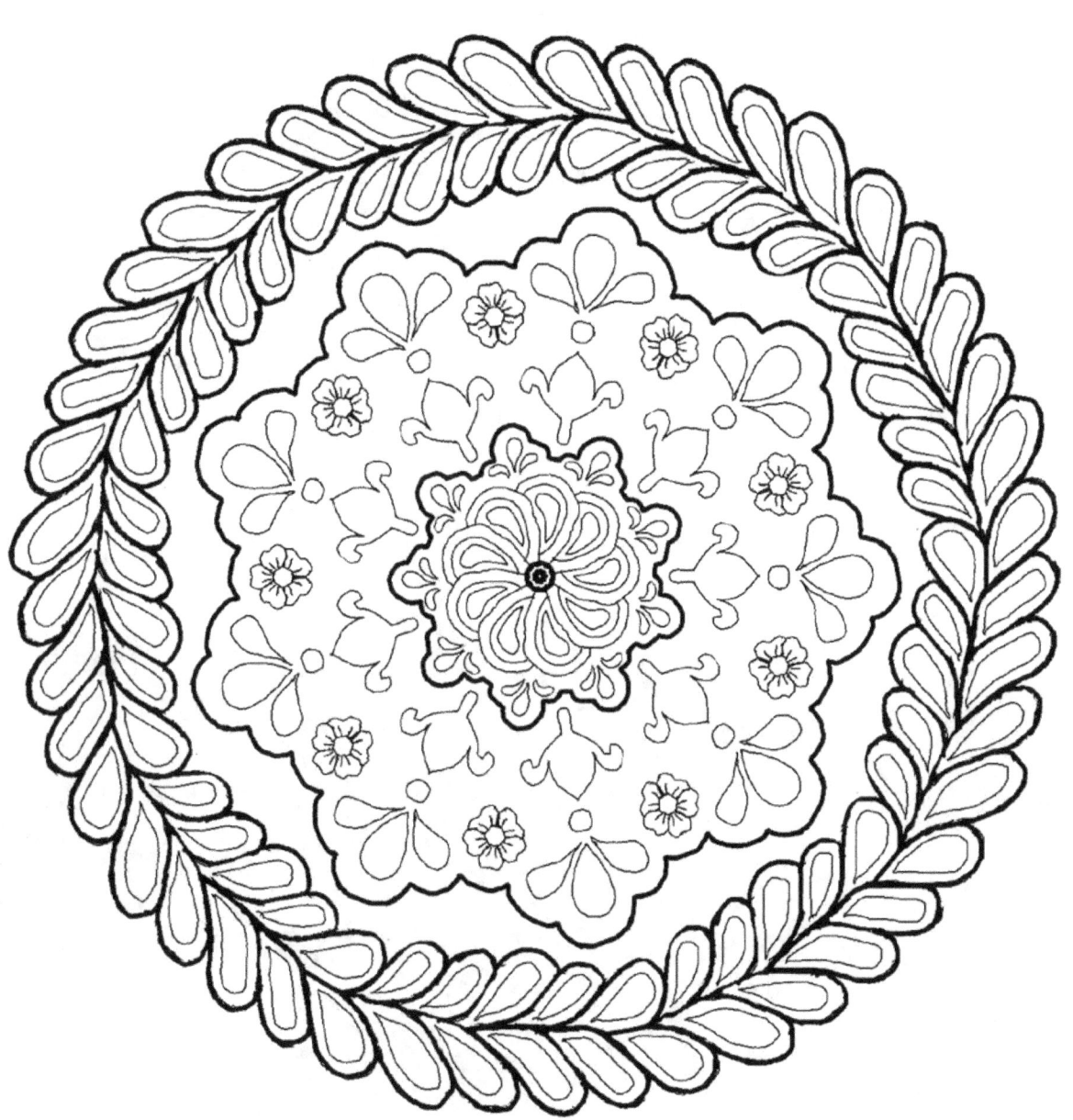

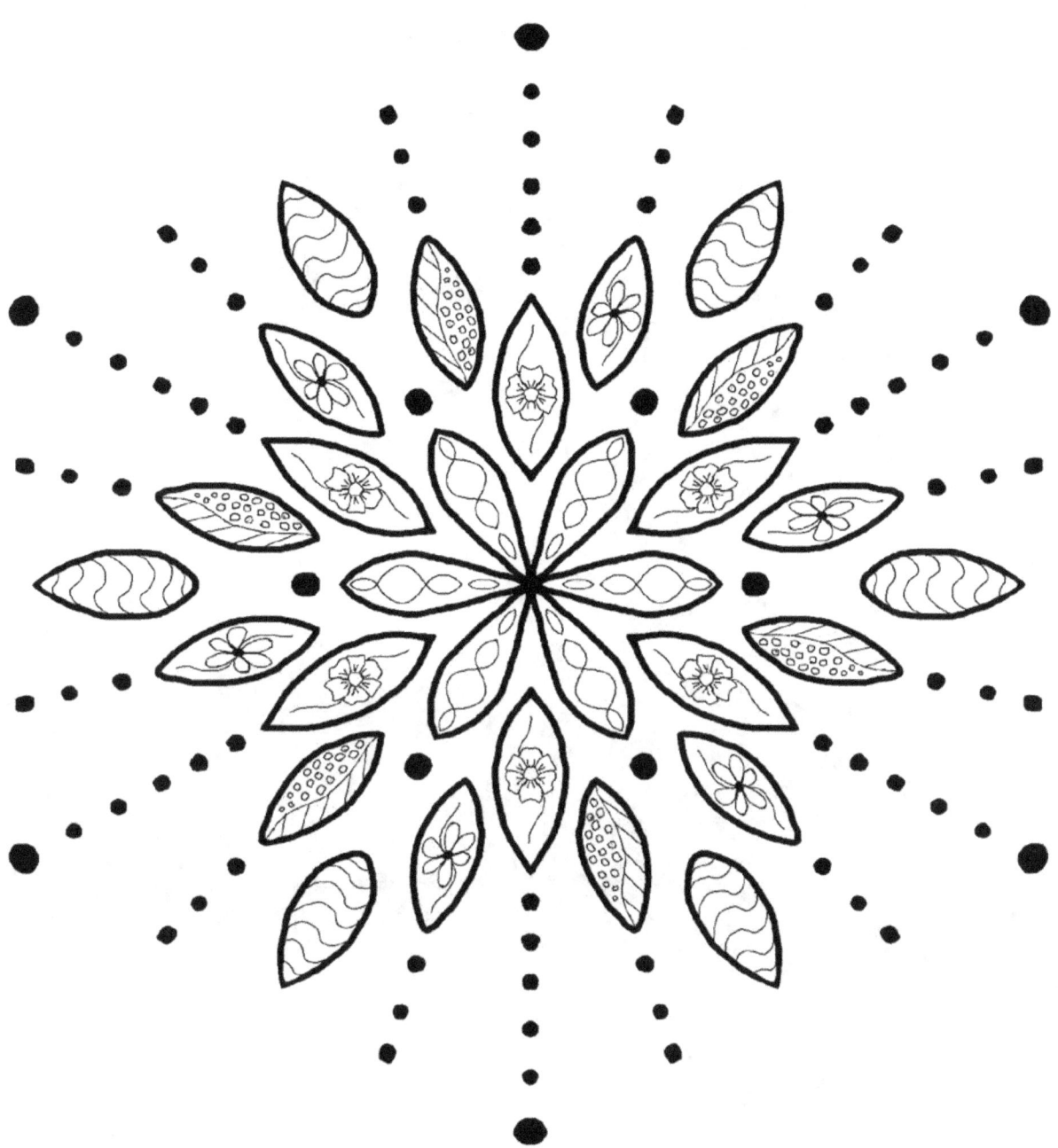

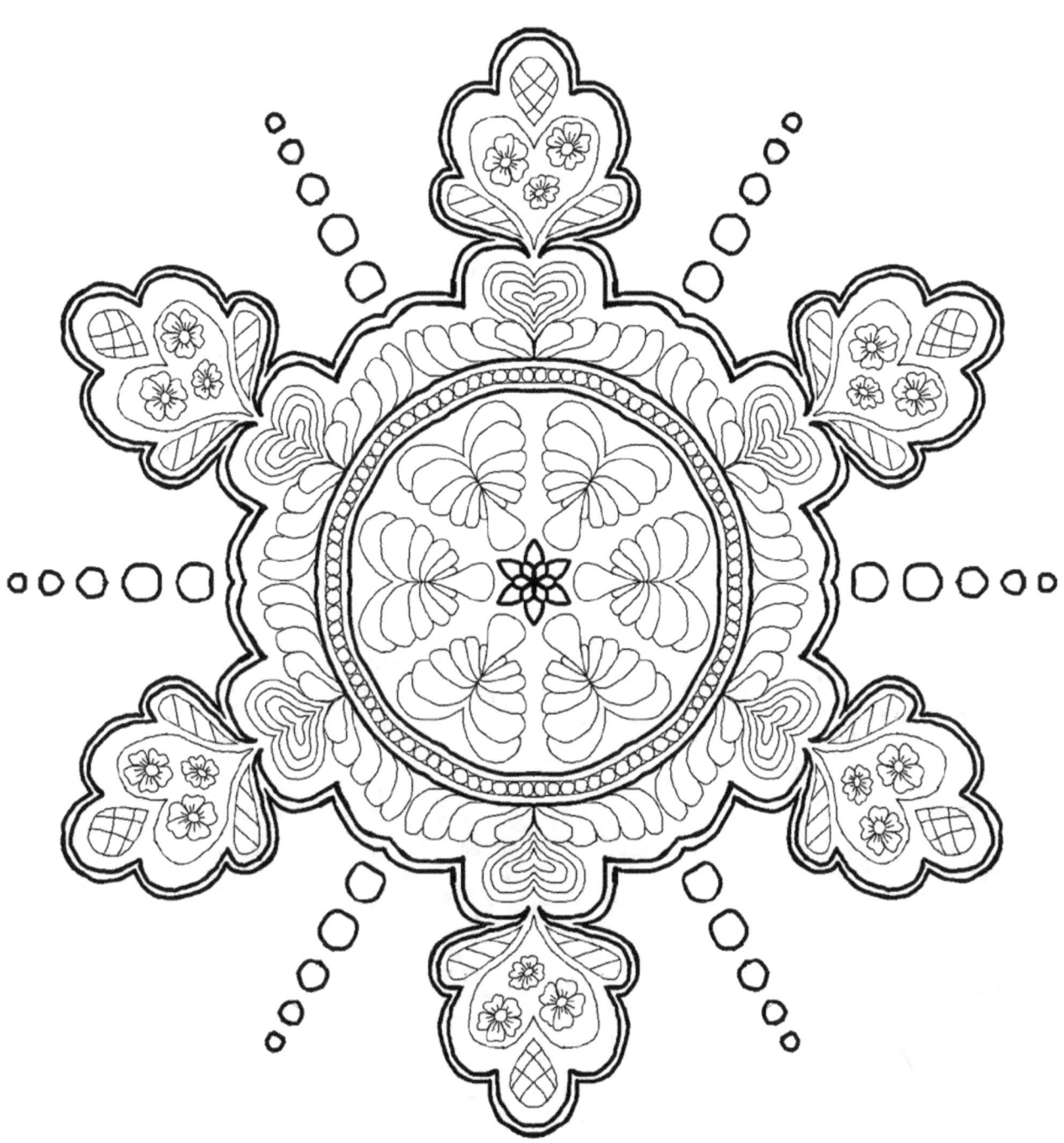

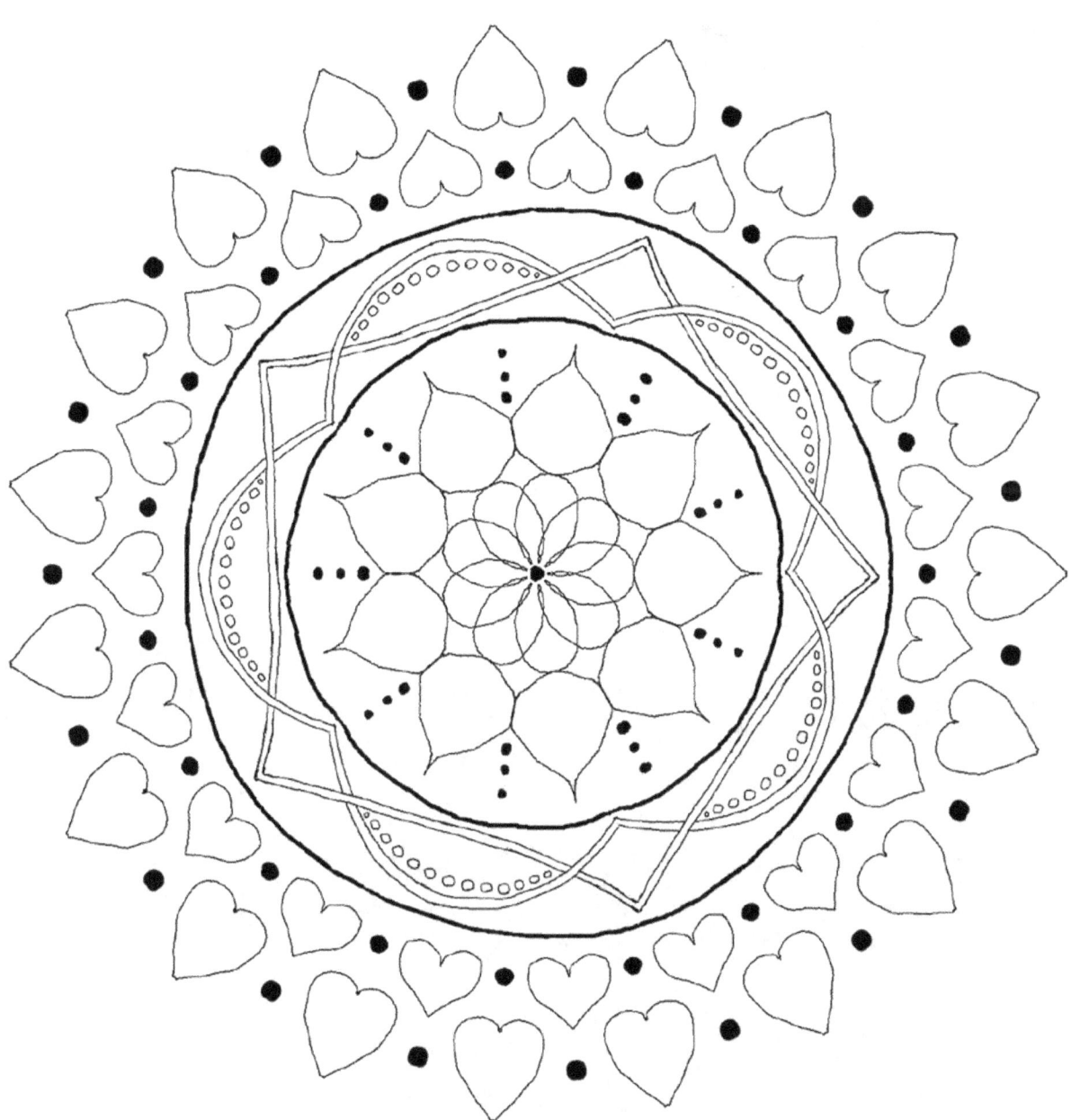

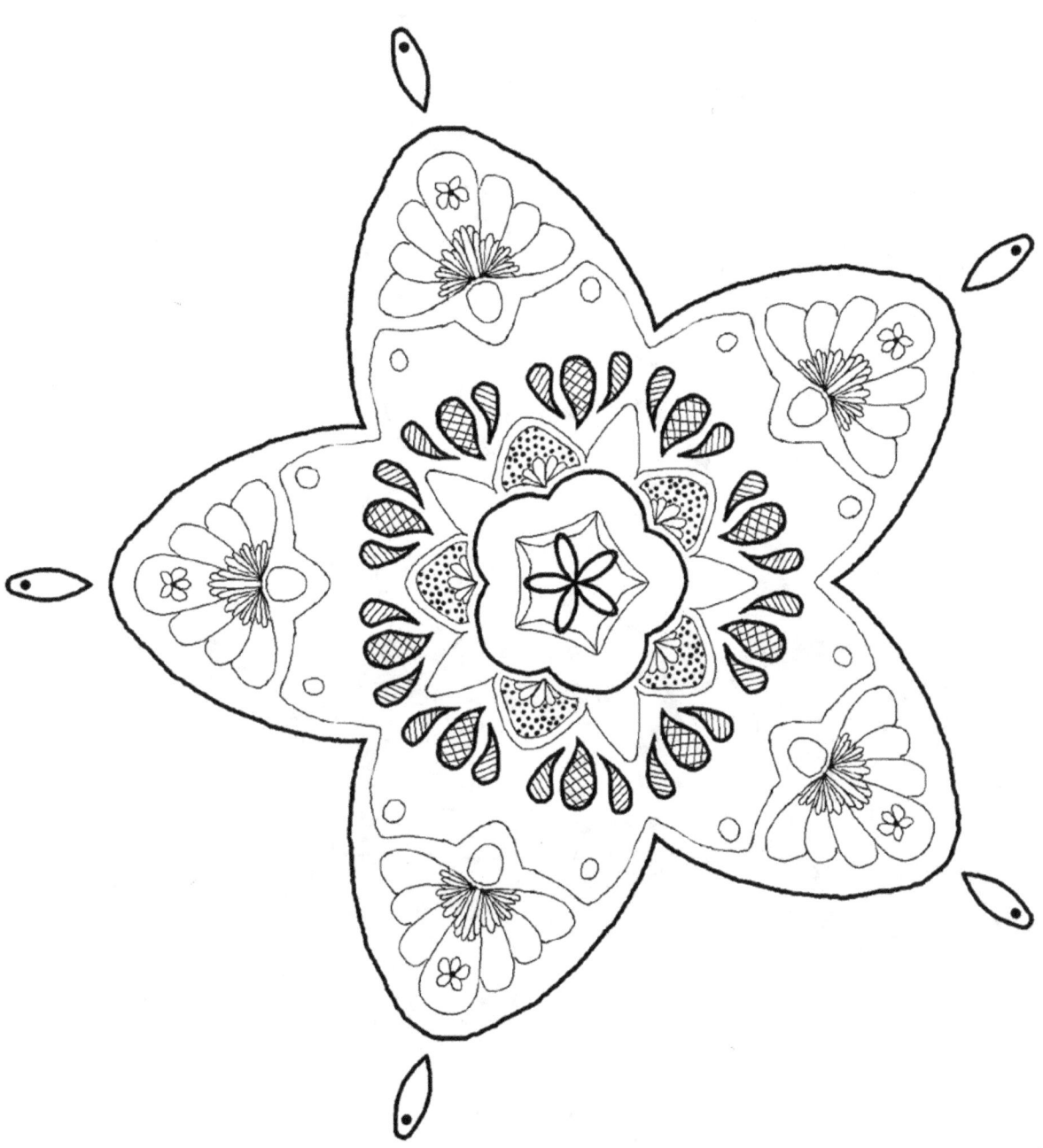

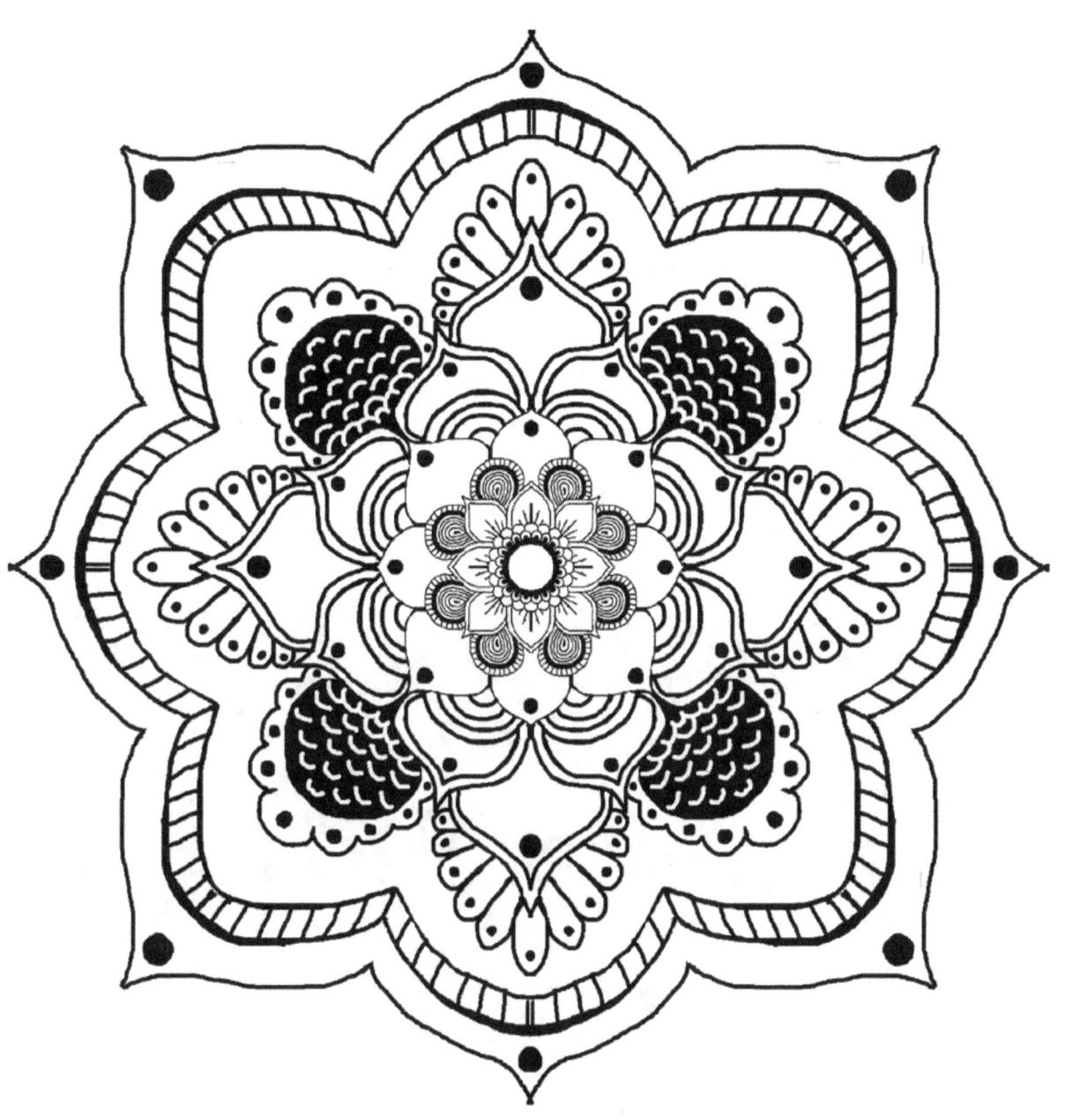

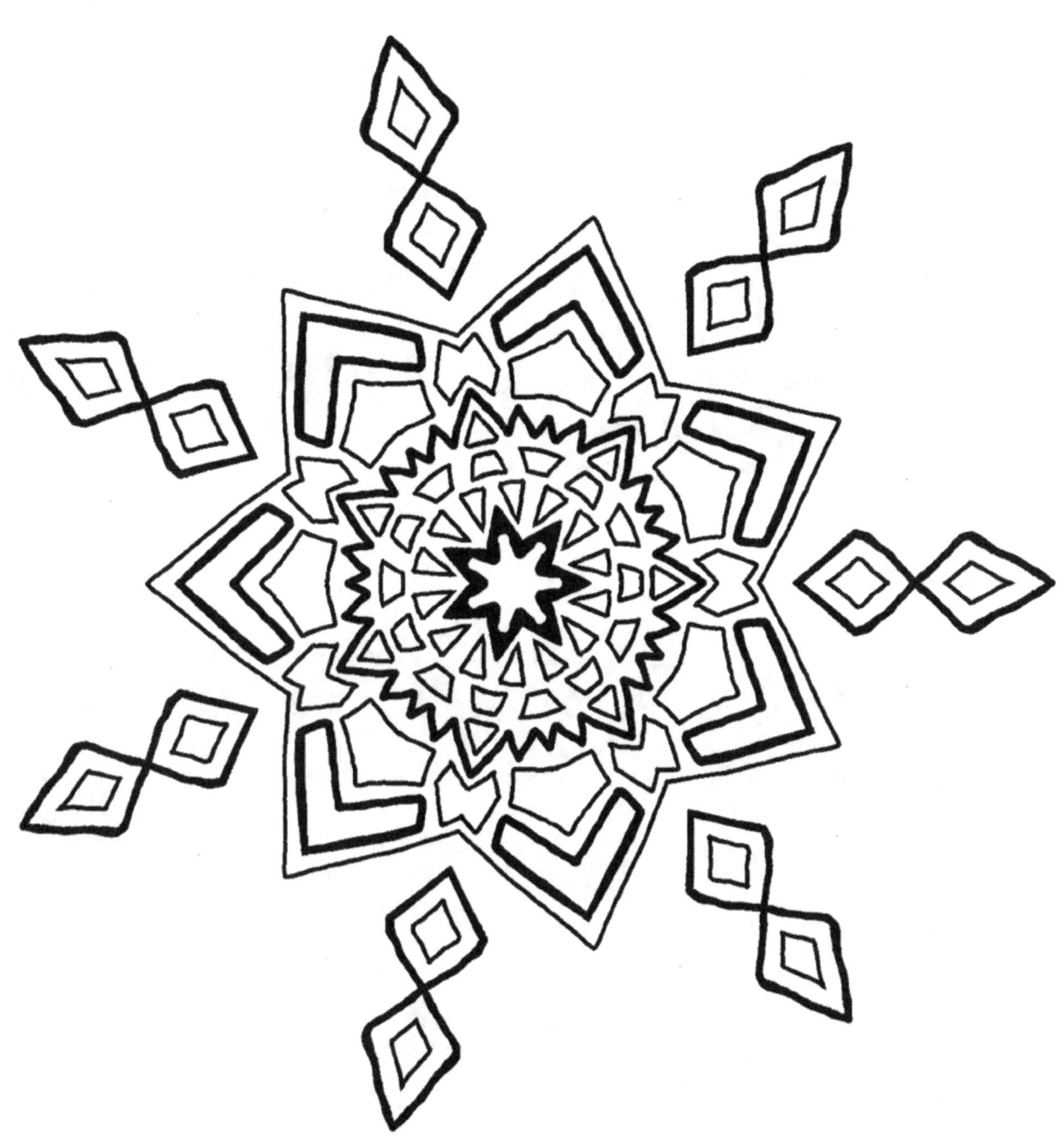

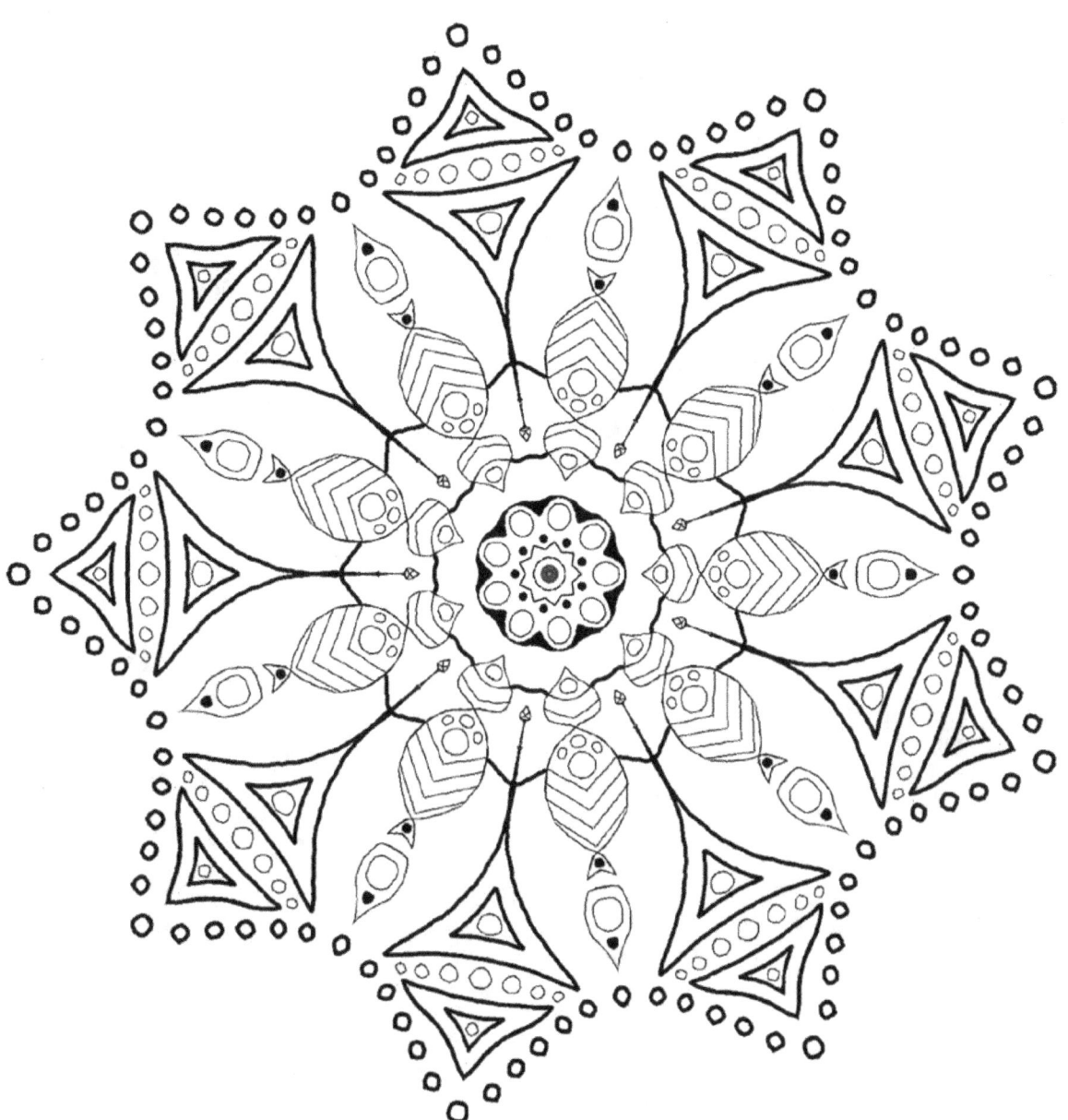

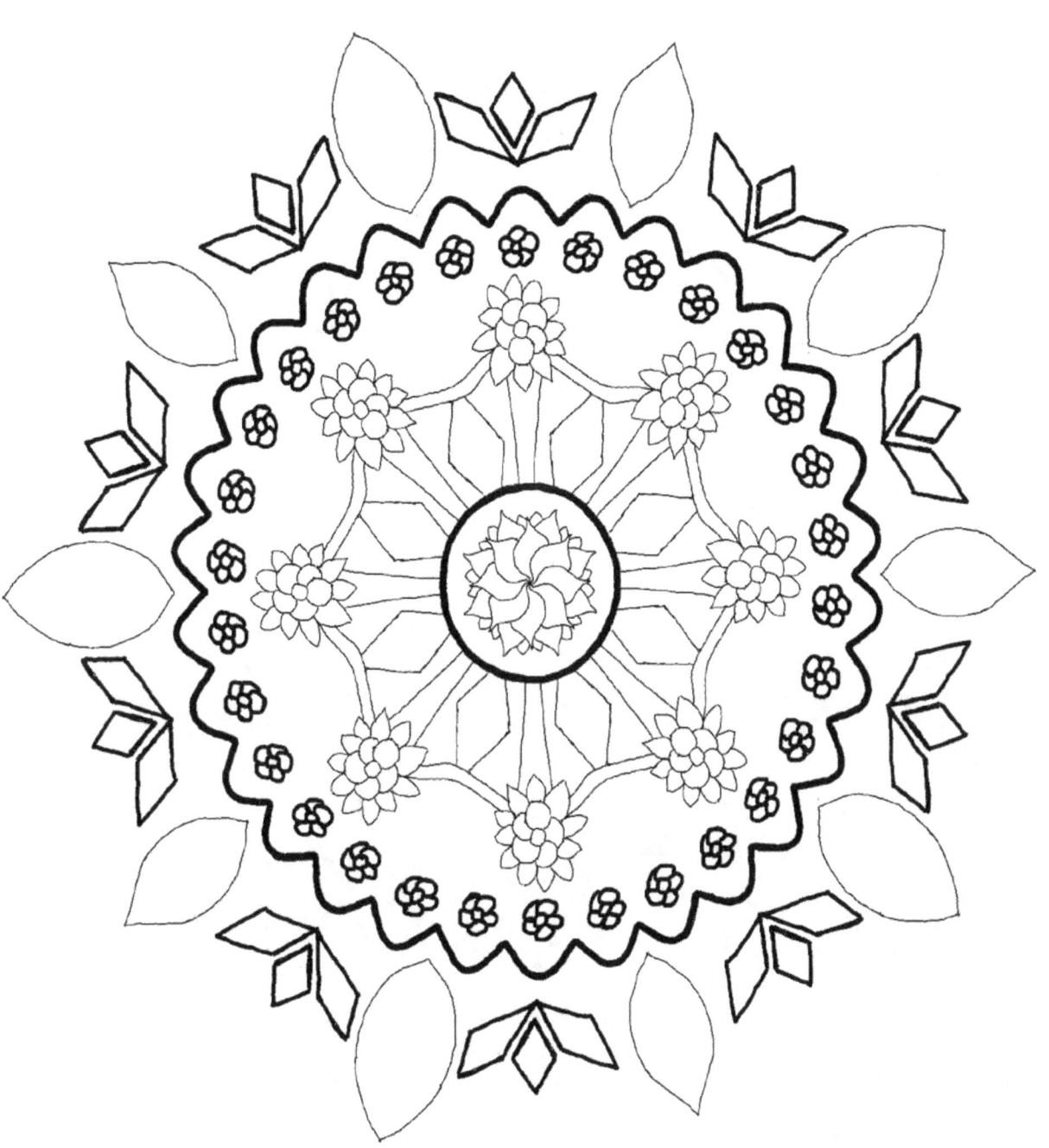

www.ingramcontent.com/pod-product-compliance
Lightning Source LLC
Chambersburg PA
CBHW081252170526
45165CB00014B/2740